ONE NATION UNDER TRUMP?

The Toxic Cult of Radical Far Right Extremists

Copyright © by Marcus Johnson

For information about permission to reproduce selections from this book, write to Marcus Johnson at mjohnson027@hotmail.com

For information about special discounts for bulk purchases, please contact Marcus Johnson at mjohnson027@hotmail.com

TABLE OF CONTENTS

Introduction……………………………………………………....4-6

Part I: DEMOCRACY IN PERIL

The American We Know……………………………….............8-17

What Once Stood As the Party Lincoln Stands No More…...18-36

A Discussion About Race, Human Rights, and Equal
Treatment………………………………………………….37-60

A Rising Generation……………………………………...61-79

Part II: ADDITIONAL ISSUES (SPEECHES)

Her Body, Her Choice, Her Freedom…………………...81-88

Guns DO Kill People……………………………………..89-97

The Roaring Lion of White Supremacy……………….98-112

The Public Trust………………………………………113-118

Conclusion……………………………………………..119-126

INTRODUCTION

Most politicians assert that they have never imagined themselves pursuing a life in politics. Many claim that God called them from a life of leisure and convenience to sacrifice on behalf of others. However, pursuing a career in public service in the effort to shine bright light on the lives of many is something I have always desired to do. It is what I have sought to do for years as an educator in both elementary and secondary schools. It is what I have done for years as a motivational speaker and an advocate against bullying and suicide. I have also done so as a first-time candidate for state representative in Louisiana's 28th District, placing second in a race against three powerful and influential candidates. In all that I do in life, I will always stand for what I know is morally just and store God, country, and people ahead of self. These are the values I learned growing up, and I work tirelessly in leading an example on behalf of those values.

I will never forget the great feelings of pride and joy as a kid watching our nation make history as we elected our first African American president, Barack Obama. It was during this moment when I knew exactly what I can accomplish, and I assume great peace in knowing that kids, adolescents, and young adults all over this country can look at my life's journey and know they can ascend to any level of greatness that their talents and hard work will ascend them. I see first-hand the uncertain crisis that has embarked upon our country. We have a situation where so many children lack greater access to education and healthcare, while countless jobs just barely keep food on the table and clothes on our children's backs. The problem of systemic injustice remains an unfortunate reality for countless people of color, women of all backgrounds, and those who identify as LGBTQ+. The longevity of the earth stands in jeopardy as a warming climate threatens our posterity. The threat of gun violence continues to rob countless lives as our leaders choose to stand idly by and do nothing. The greatest threat to our future is a radical Far Right regime headed by none other than Donald Trump, who stands willing and ready to overthrow our democracy to seize political power.

What inspires me with hope is knowing that we the American people have endured the darkest of adversities and have overcome every era of that darkness in which has come upon us. We rise above when we adhere to the best of our example. We prosper when we live up to the ideals of our nation's origin. We achieve the future when we keep our sights on what we know is critical despite the difficulty that lies ahead. This is what we do when apprehended by crisis. The adversity that has befallen our nation during the four years of Donald Trump is the most grim and dark of our lifetimes. I am deeply committed to bringing together Americans of every kind from every end of the political spectrum to reignite the engine of American democracy at full power and putting the toxic era of Donald Trump and radical Far Right extremism behind us forever. We the American people must form a movement to complete this critical task so that we can fulfill the long overdue work to increase the quality of life for every American citizen. We owe this to ourselves, our children, our grandchildren, and so on.

Part I: DEMOCRACY IN PERIL

1

THE AMERICA WE KNOW

There has never been a greater, more profound privilege in my life than to be a citizen of the United States. Only in America can a young person of color like me born in the inner-city of Chicago and raised partly in deep Southern rural Louisiana rise to any height in which he is willing to work hard to climb. Only in the United States can one rise from the deepest depths of poverty and despair to the greatest realms of promise and achievement. Only in America where that same young person of color who was bullied in school and battled depression would go on to complete four years of undergrad and eventually obtain his master's degree and become a bestselling author. In no other society on Earth are these things possible.

The only path in which to achieve greatness in many other societies is through being born into that way of life or previous affiliation with members of the nobility or those with great wealth and influence. Our systems of free enterprise, guarded with rules and a safety net for those in need, and representative democracy allow for Americans to achieve prosperity and live and speak as they please as long as no one infringes upon the human rights and well-being of others. Every generation of

Americans is summoned upon to strengthen this promise for subsequent generations. Every generation before us fulfilled the promise of passing on a greater, freer, and more equal nation onto the next generation of Americans.

WHO ARE WE?

As stated above, to be an American is a privilege in and of itself, and every citizen should be grateful. While it is our relentless insistence on limitless possibilities that makes us unique in the world, it is also our sense of identity. I refer to our American identity as to what I like to call our moral DNA, which consists of our moral character and our moral conscience. Our moral character is what calls upon each of us as individuals and all of us collectively to be decent human beings and treat one another with respect, kindness, and compassion. Our moral character calls on us to listen to each other and seek to bring out the good in our fellow Americans. It calls on us to respect and embrace those who disagree with us and still be able to work together to achieve the outcome we all desire for the country we all love. Our moral character calls on our nation's leaders to provide unity and bold leadership amid crisis and uncertainty, seeking common purpose based on shared values and intentions. Ultimately, it is our moral character that calls upon the greatest good in who we are based on our national identity and who we should strive to be as human beings.

In the face of political division, racial unrest, and moral indecency, it is our moral conscience for which summons each of us individually and all of us as a united country to condemn all these things boldly without hesitation. Our moral conscience calls upon us to condemn name-calling and the demonization of our fellow Americans because of their race or religion or sexual orientation or gender identity or political affiliation. It speaks directly to the heart of a human being when encountered with evil and reminds them of right from wrong. Our moral conscience is what propels one to be disturbed heavily by systemic injustice against people of color and women of all races and those who identity as part of the LGBTQ+ community. It calls upon us to protest peacefully in the face of police brutality that affects people of color disproportionately.

Our moral conscience instills in all of us the urgency to reject a toxic brand of leadership that emboldens the flames of hate and racism and division, that insults and mischaracterizes those who disagree with it as the enemy, that seeks to abandon democracy by overturning the results of a free and democratic election, and that tries to break the law and thwart the constitution. It calls upon our nation to heavily condemn the insurrection of violence on our Capitol that nearly resulted in the death of the former Vice-President and members of Congress. Furthermore, our moral conscience calls upon us to hold accountable the man that incited it willingly who is known as no other than Donald Trump.

This is who we are in America. Our moral DNA calls upon us to adhere to the best of ourselves and be able to stand tall and proudly against all forms of hate and injustice and moral indecency on the part of our leaders. As Americans, we must acknowledge that political rhetoric has consequences. The choice of words uttered by our nation's leaders, particularly the occupant of the Oval Office, drives the overall mood and rate of national stability. The rhetoric of our leaders will either inspire in our hearts and minds what is good and humanly decent or embolden what is wicked and that which stems from bitterness and void. Since our nation's founding in 1776, most leaders have sought to bring out the greatest in who we are as citizens. They reminded us time and time again of the beauty and pride in being an American. This was the reality when George Washington declared "I was summoned by my country, whose voice I can never hear but with veneration and love." President Lincoln sought to heal a deeply divided nation when declaring to both North and South that "We are not enemies, but we are friends; though passion may have strained, it must not break our bonds of affection."

In a nation ravaged by widespread economic despair at home and conflict abroad, President Roosevelt declared "We have learned the simple truth, as Emerson said that the only way to have a friend is to be one. We can gain no lasting peace if we approach it with suspicion or mistrust or with fear." In the quest for racial justice and equal treatment under the law, Dr. King called upon a wounded nation a hundred years after the signing of the Emancipation Proclamation to not "obtain a distrust of all white people because their presence at Lincoln's Memorial is evidence that their destiny is tied up with America's destiny." President Obama reminded us consistently that we are "one nation and one people." President Biden reminded us on the night of his victory that "We have to stop treating our opponents as our enemies. They are not our enemies. They are Americans." To hear these words from then-President-Elect Biden was a tremendous breath of fresh air for myself and millions of Americans in both parties after four dreadful years of longstanding demonization and division.

No matter what challenge or dark chapter embarks upon our journey, it must never compromise our moral DNA. Our moral DNA should never be a matter of debate; it is common sense, and it is obvious. It is the foundation of our longstanding tradition of democracy and our greater American identity. Whether or not it continues to be the compass of our national journey depends on, once again, each of us as individuals and all of us collectively as one American people.

CROSSROADS: A TIME FOR CHOOSING

After four tumultuous years of the presidency of Donald Trump, our nation finds herself at a deeply critical crossroads. We find ourselves in a dangerous predicament where our moral DNA has been compromised on the part of too many. It is of no question that former President Trump left America more divided and more politically polarized than over half a century ago. The former President consistently insulted and belittled all those who dared even to disagree with or challenge him. He emboldened the flames of hate, racism, and division to an extent for which history has not witnessed for over several decades. He told four Congresspersons of color to go back to the countries from which they came and that they had "some nerve telling us how to run our country.". The former President referred to various African countries as "shithole nations" and referred to cities with large black populations as "rat-infested ghettos." He referred consistently to the deadly COVID-19 pandemic as "the China Virus" and "KungFlu." As a first-time candidate in 2016, the former President said that Indiana-born federal judge Gonzalo Curiel was not capable of being impartial because of his "Mexican heritage."

After coming short in the 2020 Election to President Biden, Trump declared the Biden/Harris victory to be fraudulent. He did so, however, with absolutely no shred of evidence beyond a reasonable doubt. The former President continued to dumb down his supporters with baseless and ridiculous claims of election fraud because he knew they would believe them only because he said so, even in the face of no evidence beyond a reasonable doubt. He went to court over sixty times, including multiple times to the conservative-majority

Supreme Court, and got thrown out each time. Trump proceeded to coerce and threaten the Secretary of State of Georgia to "find 11,780 votes" to reverse the electoral results of that state from Biden to him. This would have been illegal in and of itself. No sitting president or candidate for the presidency in our two-hundred forty-six-year history has ever done anything of this nature. However, this would proceed to be only the tip of the tentacle.

When Congressional and Senatorial leaders met on January 6th, 2021 to make the certification of the 2020 Election official, then-President Trump incited a dangerous insurrectional surge on the Capitol that resulted in multiple deaths of and injuries in law enforcement officials and resulted nearly in the death of members of Congress and the Senate as well as then-Vice President Mike Pence. During Trump's address to the mob that would storm the Capitol, he declared that "We will never take back our country with weakness. We need to fight like hell because if we don't, we will no longer have a country." He would then encourage them to march to the Capitol. In addition to the former President's dangerous encouragement of violence, Rudy Giuliani would utter the words "trial by combat," followed by Representative Mo Brooks urging the mob to "Kick ass! Kick ass!" The radical Far Right extremists who marched to and stormed the Capitol in the name of Donald Trump were chanting "Hang Mike Pence! Hang Mike Pence!" They were also chanting racial slurs to black police officers and physically attacked members of law enforcement.

At every opportunity given, Donald Trump would wield the power of his authority to embolden what is the absolute worst in the character of too many. He spoke directly to their hate and bigoted ideologies to achieve his own political goals and inflate his own ego. What was a hundred times worse was watching his own party either stand idly by or be complicit in his toxic methods every step of the way. It was disheartening watching Senators Lindsay Graham and Mitch McConnell and former UN Ambassador Nikki Haley stand toe to toe with an individual who has put himself before the country time and time again. It was deeply disheartening to watch countless individuals continue to support such a diabolical, narcissistic figure for the nation's highest office who possesses extraordinarily little to no moral decency in clear conscience. I was astonished deeply over the fact that so many were allowing themselves to be conned so greatly to the point where all moral conscience had been compromised. Moral character is completely anathema to Donald Trump's character and stood opposite to his presidency. Moral conscience was overtaken by passion driven by moral indecency.

We have reached a point in our country where one side demonizes the other as the enemy. We nearly succumbed to what modern history will recall as the most dark and dangerous path ever traveled by the American people. Our democracy faces grave threats of untold proportions. If we as an American people ever reached a milestone in our country where demonizing those who disagree with us as our enemies becomes the norm, we will lose what we know as a nearly three-century tradition of democracy. If we no longer sit aside our personal feelings and admiration for a political figure for the betterment of the country, America as human civilization knows her will cease to exist. President Lincoln declared that "While the people retain their virtue and their vigilance, no administration by any extreme of wickedness or folly can seriously injure the government in the short span of four years." If President Lincoln, the first Republican to serve as Commander-in-Chief, were alive today, he would acknowledge that former President Donald Trump did just that in excess.

The core base of the Republican Party has succumbed to a toxic narcissistic ideology that is championed by radical Far Right extremists and built on narrow-minded bigotry and baseless conspiracy theories. It stands in stark contrast to everything we as Americans hold sacred and all that we as human beings should know to be good and decent. It would be accurate historically to assert that the dark era brought to us by Donald Trump would call for what President Reagan, another admirable figure among most Republicans, coined in 1964 as "A Time for Choosing." As dark and dreary as this toxic era of Trumpism stands, it is unmatched to the unyielding and forever abiding power of Americanism. I believe with all my heart that the true greatness that has always defined our very existence will rise above and endure for all of eternity. We as the American people must uphold our moral DNA, which consists of moral character for which propels us to our greatest humanly good and guarded by moral conscience that moves us to reject evil and all that is beneath what is good and decent. America's moral DNA must push forward, and our democracy must thrive.

2

WHAT ONCE STOOD AS THE PARTY OF LINCOLN STANDS NO MORE

One of the most important aspects of our democracy is the ability to share a healthy balance of ideas and vision with those in which we disagree. Our ability to conduct a civil debate concerning the issues important to us all and come together as one American people has been the lifeblood of this wonderful country of ours for over two and a half centuries. Our Founders debated for months until they were finally able to craft a constitution that made a newborn nation the most unique in the entire history of human civilization. What enabled our Founders to accomplish this was both their ability and choosing to unite with common purpose despite their vast disagreements. Yes, they shared great differences in vision and methods, but their goals and motives were very much the same. The aim of their goals and motives was to establish a country built on self-government. This is the idea that all individuals should be free and in control of their own destiny as long as no one infringes upon the well-being of others.

Over the course of two and a half centuries, Americans of both parties have always united with common effort to make the promises of our Founders a greater reality for every subsequent generation. This is part of who we are as Americans. We debate passionately over the critical issues that affect the lives of us all and come together in the end to forge a vision to move our country forward. Democrats and Republicans alike have held true to these historical and moral truths. However, as discussed in the previous chapter, this longstanding democratic tradition of our republic stands in a moment of great peril and uncertainty. To truly put an end to the dark and dangerous division brought to us by toxic leadership and restore the soul of representative democracy, we must acknowledge the path that led us here from the beginning.

THE G.O.P. (GRAND OLD PARTY OF LINCOLN)

Upon the drafting of our constitution, various political parties would emerge and lead the governance of a young but powerful nation. As our nation continued to expand from birthhood, the grave sin of slavery remained a bitter, harsh reality for African Americans. This was a time in America when people of color were recognized broadly as property. People of color were acknowledged as no more than three-fifths of citizens in the eyes of the law. The reality of the livelihoods of blacks exceeded no place beyond the scope of labor and the plantation. This was the case for nearly four centuries; the grave sin of slavery preceded our nation's birth by nearly three centuries. It was not until the emergence of the Kansas-Nebraska Act when the tide began to shift. This act legalized slavery in both the Kansas and Nebraska territories and would allow them both to become slave states.

Many abolitionists began to voice strong opposition to the new law. This same group of abolitionists, consisting of both blacks and whites, would meet at a schoolhouse in Ripon, Wisconsin on March 20, 1854, and form what we know today as the Republican Party. The G.O.P., as it is referred to quite frequently, formed to abolish slavery in its entirety. These early onset Republicans asserted that no individual should be subjected to the chains of bondage and oppression. The ideas of national unity and fair and equal treatment for all were the bedrock of early Republican philosophy. These simple but powerful ideas would begin to be transformed into reality during the presidency of the first Republican president, Abraham Lincoln. President Lincoln's signing of the Emancipation Proclamation would only begin to fulfill the promise of liberty for countless slaves who deserved nothing less than to experience that liberty to the fullest. Much more work would be required in advancing the true promise of liberty and justice for all.

During this time in American history, the G.O.P. was a spearhead for civil rights and equal treatment. There would be the establishment of the Thirteenth, Fourteenth, and Fifteenth Amendments to the Constitution, which abolished slavery forever, established citizenship for all native-born persons from this country, and extended voting rights to men of every race, respectively. Briefly, Republican president Rutherford B. Hayes stood boldly for civil rights in the late Nineteenth Century. Regarding the issue of slavery, Hayes was a staunch abolitionist who declared that "desperate diseases require desperate remedies." As governor of the state of Ohio, he saw the ratification from his state of the Fifteenth Amendment. To become president, however, Hayes sold out his allegiance to greater liberty to Southern Dixiecrats by promising to pull troops out of the South and end Reconstruction efforts, which foresaw nearly a century of Jim Crow segregation, lynchings, and widespread discrimination.

President Eisenhower signed into law the 1957 and 1960 Civil Rights Acts that provided federal protection for voting rights. It was Eisenhower who sent federal troops to Little Rock Central High School in Little Rock, Arkansas when nine black students were prevented from integrating the school. Senator Barry Goldwater of Arizona, who was a member of both the NAACP and National Urban League and an active supporter of desegregation in Phoenix, worked successfully to desegregate the Arizona Air National Guard when he was the air liaison officer. This was done two years before the national military was desegregated. While Goldwater did not support the 1964 Civil

Rights Act, which he should have done so with no hesitation, he did support the 1957 and 1960 Acts along with most other Republicans in Congress at the time. As the second half of the Twentieth Century had begun to unfold, the G.O.P. became alarmingly oblivious to the issues of race and civil rights.

The quest to fulfill the work began by President Lincoln in the 1860s to spread liberty and bring the country closer together was a longstanding democratic tradition that was strongly intact. Responding to crisis with razor thin urgency and uniting in our darkest hours were longstanding American rituals that we always kept sacred. This has forever led us forward and made us stronger. Many of us never once thought or imagined the day in America when the very principles that define our greatness would nearly cease to exist.

AND HERE CAME DONALD TRUMP...

For as long as history can remember, the Republican Party has always portrayed itself to be the party of patriotism, unity, equality, and moralism. Over the course of the Twentieth Century, ideals such as human virtue and the strength of the family would also become fundamental components of the Republican banner. This platform, the Party of Lincoln, would define the rhetoric of Republican leaders as well as the goal of Republican domestic and foreign policy.

Republican leaders such as Abraham Lincoln, Teddy Roosevelt, Dwight Eisenhower, Colin Powell, and John McCain applied the Republican banner in such a way that would garner deep respect and admiration that crossed party lines. While President Reagan was very insensitive to the cause of racial equality, which should never be ignored, he portrayed a deep and abiding sense of patriotism that extended national pride into the hearts of Americans in both parties. When Reagan spoke of the transfer of power in his first inaugural address, he declared "this every four-year ceremony we accept as normal is nothing less than a miracle." Proceeding to thank his predecessor, President Carter, he declared,

> "Mr. President, I want our fellow citizens to know how much you did to carry on this tradition. By your gracious cooperation in the transition process, you have shown a watching world that we are a united people, pledged to maintaining a political system which guarantees individual liberty to a greater degree than any other. I want to thank you and your people for all your help in maintaining the continuity, which is the bulwark of our republic."

Furthermore, the party of Lincoln seemed to hold sacred to America's moral DNA. All of this began to rip apart at the seams with the presidential candidacy of a man whose character and rhetoric are completely antithetical to all that the party of Lincoln has once presented itself to be. His choice of character also contradicts America's character, and this narcissistic choice of moral indecency belongs to no other than Donald John Trump. Donald Trump will go down in history as by far the worst president the United States has ever had. He led America down the most dark and uncertain path in modern history. As president, he insulted and belittled anyone who dared even to give the slightest hint of disagreement or critique, whether the person was a Republican or Democrat. The way he would attack free press and speak to journalists, particularly female ones, was deplorable. In addition to the insurrection of violence on our Capitol, the worst act of former President Trump was successfully appealing to a deep seated racial and xenophobic bigotry and hate held in the hearts of too many. This is a group of individuals I refer to as the radical Far Right, which consists of a substantial bulk of those who supported Trump consistently.

The radical Far Right is a group of individuals that subscribe to a philosophy that asserts that anyone or anything that is not like it is deemed inferior or un-American. These individuals are bothered by the fact that America is more inclusive, diverse, multiracial, and multicultural than she has ever been. They are bothered by immigrants coming to our country to seek a better life. When Donald Trump referred to those coming from Mexico as "rapists and drug dealers and criminals," those on the Far Right were told exactly what they wanted to hear. Building a wall along the America-Mexico border was something very delightful for the Far Right. These individuals see immigrants as people who are trying to take over this country.

The radical Far Right in this country subscribes to a white supremacist ideology that adamantly opposes the ideas of greater diversity and equal treatment under the law. The Far Right radicals who were shouting derogatory statements about Jews while rioting in Charlottesville over the tearing down of Confederate statues were honored and pleased when former President Trump declared that there were "very fine people on both sides." So according to Donald Trump, white supremacists are fine people. This is the reason it took him countless months through deep racial tension to finally condemn white supremacy, which was a pure delight for the radical Far Right and just a slap in a face to the rest of us. When Trump referred to the term Black Lives Matter as a "symbol of hate," he spoke directly to the heart of the Far Right. Instead of condemning the unlawful murders of George Floyd and Jacob Blake and Breonna Taylor as well as the sin of systemic racism altogether, he condemned the movement to eliminate injustice from our country.

Personally, I was bothered deeply to see many on the Right remain silent after the brutally unlawful murder of George Floyd. When individuals were tearing down statues of racist confederate slave owners, however, they became offended and outraged. Then the former President came out in favor of a ten-year felony for anyone who assumes a role in tearing down a confederate statue. Instead of favoring a felony for law enforcement officers who unlawfully murder individuals or abuse their authority, he instead went after those who were angry over the state of injustice. This is the same president who said he believed that both the confederate flag and statues are a "source of Southern pride and heritage." The former President was continually active and consistent in racist rhetoric and behavior.

The Radical Right, whose followers consist of direct descendants of a deeply embedded spirit of Jim Crow, is opposed deeply to any efforts to reverse the systemic racism that is the result of centuries of racial injustice. Responses to efforts to overturn decades of institutional injustice include "re-writing history," "reverse discrimination," "just more and more socialism," "slavery ended a long time ago," or "nothing is ever enough for them." When one calls out bigoted statements or racial injustice, the Far Right will go so far as to accuse that person of being the true racist or unpatriotic or simply living in the past. This has, in fact, happened to me personally on social media. After writing a status on Facebook condemning the term "China virus," coined by former President Trump, some of my former conservative friends accused me of being the true racist. After a back-and-forth debate, some of them either deleted me as a friend or blocked me altogether. Because I knew in my heart that I was applying moral conscience, I was not bothered over losing them. I was also not bothered because my former friends only revealed their own deeply embedded racism.

Another former friend of mine wrote a status on Facebook stating, "Since Trevor Noah hates America so much, maybe he should go back to South Africa." The post was met with widespread condemnation and would be taken down eventually. This is parallel to what former President Trump said for four Congresspersons of color to do. He said they should "go back to the countries from which they came." He went on to say they "had some nerve telling us how to run our country." This is something that no sitting American president has ever done, and the "us" he was referring to are those who believe that anyone who is not white, straight, cisgender, a professed Christian, and native-born are inferior. This is what Donald Trump appeals to, and he made many of those who are racist and xenophobic comfortable enough to express their hate openly. He also appealed to a deep sense of Islamophobia in his base with a travel ban on Muslims.

Long into the Trump presidency, I can recall personally witnessing so many becoming as comfortable and bold as to apply the N word on social media and refer to people of color as lazy and worthless and thuggish. My friend Rebecca, who owns a take-out restaurant from home, was attacked racially on Facebook by a guy who had a Trump 2020 frame in his profile picture. A former school board member in my old district shared a post on Facebook that stated that all of those who support the Black Lives Matter movement should give up their EBT cards and government assistance. He resigned from his seat shortly after a vast array of condemnation. A former elementary school teacher in my former district was fired for commenting on a post that Black Lives Matter activists should be hung from a rope. I also witnessed many people in various Facebook groups with the Trump 2020 picture frame using the N word and other derogatory attacks on people of color. While I did see some of this seldomly prior to the Trump era, it became far more frequent long into his tenure. This is not just a coincidence or some argument on the part of the Democrats; it is reality. I have witnessed it for myself and so has countless others.

Former President Trump's divisive, cruel, and hateful rhetoric through the consistent use of dog whistling spoke directly to the hate and bigotry in the hearts of those who oppose all who is the opposite of them. This narcissistic ideology led America to a place that is unrecognizable. Given all that had taken place during the Trump presidency, what tops the cake is that top Republican leaders have either followed in Trump's footsteps or simply chose to not reject his toxic leadership. Representative Steve King of Iowa asked, "When did white nationalism become a bad thing?" Furthermore, many Republican leaders in Congress and the Senate continued to cheer on the former President despite his iniquities. Senator Mitt Romney, who was the 2012 Republican nominee for president, is now an enemy within the G.O.P. simply because he had the courage to condemn

Trump's morally indecent behavior and dangerous leadership. Representative Liz Cheney was removed as Chairperson of the Republican House Conference because she rejected the myth that the 2020 Election was stolen and chooses to stand up to the former President. Senator Bill Cassidy, who has maintained a consistent conservative voting record during his tenure in the Senate, is now another enemy for holding the former President accountable. There was footage of Senator Lindsay Graham of South Carolina getting harassed and screamed at as he was boarding a plane for choosing to support the certification of President Biden's victory after the insurrectionist surge on the Capitol. Senator Graham, however, re-joined the toxic cult.

I have personally read the comments on social media condemning former Senators Kelly Loeffler and, again, Bill Cassidy for fulfilling their constitutional duty to vote to certify the 2020 Election results. The radical Far Right has accused former Vice President Pence of committing treason and referred to him as a traitor for simply abiding by the Constitution and not breaking the law. America watched as Far Right extremists stormed the Capitol and threatened the loss of life of our leaders. We heard them as they were chanting "hang Mike Pence!" "Hang Mike Pence!" The insurrection on Capitol Hill could have been prevented if the former President had done his job and conceded defeat to then-President-Elect Biden like all those who came before him had done. Instead, he attempted to break the law, spread lies and baseless conspiracy theories supported by the radical Far Right group QAnon, and incite a deadly insurrection on the Capitol, leaving deep wounds in our democracy. It did not help that many in the party stood at his side and forwarded baseless conspiracy theories. If Lincoln or Roosevelt or Eisenhower or John McCain were alive to see what the Republican Party has become and its effect on the country, they would be disappointed gravely.

All of those in the Republican Party who represented the best of America would never stand for what Donald Trump has done, and they would have fought with every fiber of their existence to prevent this toxic era from ever taking place. Specifically concerning the late Senator John McCain, he proved over the course of his entire career to be a person of astounding integrity. In every opportunity given, he upheld our moral DNA. When a supporter at a rally asked if then-Senator Barack Obama is an Arab, he responded how any honest and humble individual would do so: "No, ma'am. Senator Obama is a decent family man and citizen with whom I just happen to have fundamental disagreements with on certain issues, and that's what this campaign is all about." He did not use that moment as a political opportunity to demonize his opponent like Donald Trump would have done in a heartbeat. After losing to then-President-Elect Obama, he humbly and gracefully conceded defeat and pledged unity. He proceeded even as far as to acknowledge Booker T. Washington being the first African American to enter the White House and have coffee with President Teddy Roosevelt. He used that moment to celebrate America's election of the first person of color to the presidency as a source of pride and joy. He reminded us of the power of our democracy and its enormous rewards.

We all know what Donald Trump chose to do after losing to then-President-Elect Biden. He continued a nasty tirade of lies and baseless claims of fraud for three and a half months, which only drove a divided nation into deeper chaos. What did most of those in his party do? Many of those in his party cheered him on either because they believed the hype or were afraid of Trump's radical base. By accepting the results of the election, the Far Right base would condemn them as the enemy only because it went against Trump. This demonstrates the clear difference between the character of men like the late great Senator John McCain and disgraced former President Donald Trump. It also demonstrates the difference between individuals like Senator McCain and those who stood by Donald Trump considering his toxic behavior. Any Republican should have had no problem putting the country and moral decency over their personal feelings and/or admiration for Trump. This is what true patriotism calls on each of us to do. This is what so many before us would have done in the blink of an eye.

Pledging allegiance to a political figure over the country out of fear of enmity from his base is not patriotic. This is the kind of behavior that would take place in a dictatorship. When citizens of Germany tried to oppose Hitler, they were either killed or placed in a forced labor camp. This was the case in the former Soviet Union when citizens opposed Stalin. Tens of millions of individuals lost their lives, while others lost their freedom. What transpired during the Trump presidency far exceeds our character. It far exceeds our moral DNA where our moral conscience calls on us to reject such evil and malice. The Republican Party has failed tremendously and miserably in doing so. The core base of the party now consists of a toxic narcissistic ideology championed by the Far Right, which had been emboldened like never before by Donald Trump. Anyone who calls out and condemns the evil will be deemed the enemy or as inferior or un-American. This toxic Far Right ideology is referred to as Trumpism. Trumpism is anything but conservative and certainly not American.

The longstanding consequence of Trumpism is the ultimate and absolute obsoletion of American democracy in its entirety. This would lead to an outright inability for us to work together as a country. Trumpism would lead to the ultimate collapse of confidence in our voting system because half the country will just assume there was widespread fraud if its candidate were to lose an election, even if there is not a shred of evidence beyond a reasonable doubt to prove such a dangerous claim. The outcome of Trumpism in America would be civil war. If former President Trump had won a second term, the prospects for civil war would have been greater than any of us could imagine. The worst thing that we could do as Americans is tell ourselves that it could never happen. It is happening right now as election lies are continuing to be spread and as states are passing laws attacking voting rights and human rights and a woman's right to choose. The next worst thing we could do is ignore the vitality of the deliberate attack on our democracy and the prospects for an endless political stalemate.

I wholeheartedly condemn all of those who were calling for secession after the former President lost his bid for a second term. One of those voices belonged to former Texas G.O.P. Chair, Lt. Col. Allen West. His precise words were, "Maybe a handful of states who believes in upholding the Constitution should go off and form our own union." This is the same man who has quoted President Lincoln on multiple occasions and applauded him and his party for abolishing slavery. He also condemned former southern Democrats for seceding from the Union following the Civil War. Praising Lincoln and the party that ended slavery and calling for Southern secession is a clear contradiction. The cost of emancipating countless African Americans from the bondage of slavery was, in fact, secession, which is the very thing Lincoln and the early-on Republicans were fighting so desperately to prevent.

For former Texas G.O.P. Chairperson Allen West to assert that our country should once again break up into North and South just because his party lost the 2020 Presidential Election is beyond disgraceful and only further proof that demonstrates how far the Republican Party of today has drifted from the original party that formed in 1854. The party that ended slavery and spearheaded the civil rights movement has become the party that champions racist rhetoric and behavior and dismisses systemic racism as a hoax. The party that gave us the Thirteenth, Fourteenth, and Fifteenth Amendments to the Constitution is now the party that is attempting to stifle America's most sacred right to vote and take us back into the 1950s. The party that once called for national unity amid civil war and secession now deems anyone who opposes Trump the enemy. The party that once adhered to the highest degree of patriotism now pledges allegiance to a political figure over moral conscience and love of country. The party that once stored moral decency on the highest pedestal now refuses to call out and reject morally indecent behavior, whether it is taking place in the Oval Office or throughout the country in the form of injustice. The party that has always pledged to stand tall for family values is now a party that downplays a deadly national pandemic, refuses to extend relief to families in need, and refuses to give every American worker a livable wage to support their family. The party that would have taken the threats of climate change with fierce urgency is now the party that dismisses the drastic impact on the long-term health of our planet.

Instead of holding the former President accountable for inciting the deadly insurrection on the Capitol, Republicans in the Senate gave him a pass. Instead of condemning Congressperson Majorie Taylor-Greene for harassing victims of the

Parkland shooting and calling for the execution of Democratic leaders, the party is condemning all of those who voted with conscience to impeach Donald Trump. The party of Lincoln is gone; it has been replaced with something that is extremely dangerous. The toxic cult of Donald Trump and radical Far Right extremism has no place in American politics and must be defeated. It is defeated when Americans go out and vote in historically record numbers in every presidential, congressional, senatorial, and gubernatorial election. It is defeated when Americans mobilize in their communities and support candidates who will stand tall for democracy and pledge to fight for working families. It happens when we fight for what makes this country great and unique.

With the newly elected President Biden and Vice President Harris brings tremendous hope and a huge breath of fresh air. Defeating Trumpism, however, remains a broad and fundamental task before the nation. I have one-hundred percent faith in our ability to overcome the deepest root of evil. Putting the toxic era of Trumpism behind our nation forever and restoring American democracy at full strength are tasks that we as Americans can and must fulfill. As we begin this important journey in America, let us heed the words of President Eisenhower: "If a political party does not have its foundation in the determination to advance a cause that is right and that is moral, then it is not a political party; it is merely a conspiracy to seize power."

As the Republican Party of today continues to worship the coattails of Donald Trump, dismiss the unfortunate realities endured by countless Americans, refuse to support ladders of opportunity for all citizens, and expand the assault on millions of Americans' sacred right to vote, it will go down in history as merely a conspiracy to seize power. If the G.O.P. refuses to unite with the rest of the country and instead insists on continuing the bandwagon of hate speech, threats of violence, closed-minded thinking, and the spread of misinformation, it needs to simply step aside and stop wasting America's time. All of those who truly love our country will never store admiration for any political figure over love of country, apply the Constitution only when it is politically convenient, and divide the American people, but I implore the Republican Party to re-direct its course and reclaim a lasting commitment to the country we all love.

3

A DISCUSSION ABOUT RACE, HUMAN RIGHTS, AND EQUAL TREATMENT

All of us as Americans are greatly aware of the deep state of division that currently holds over our beloved nation. While we can acknowledge that the toxic leadership of the Trump administration had both a massive and unprecedented effect on our divisions, its roots are deeply seated and far precede our generation. They also precede the generation before ours and the generation before that. The deep state of division in America exists in terms of race, gender identity, sexual orientation, and sometimes religion. Too often, unjust laws and discriminatory practices against certain groups of Americans will cause many to perceive these groups in a negative perspective, which only makes it more difficult for us all to see one another. This was the reality through nearly four centuries of slavery, followed by an additional one hundred years of Jim Crow segregation and violence. This is also true for the LGBTQ+ community in the face of hate crimes as well as unacceptable unjust laws and practices.

So many of those who came before us such as Rosa Parks and Dr. Martin Luther King, Jr.

fought fiercely day and night and gave their all to see every one of God's children be regarded with the dignity and respect they deserve as human beings. They fought adamantly so that every American enjoys the right to exist in a free society. They protested in the streets, held sit-ins, endured the dog attacks and beatings at the hands of law enforcement, went to jail, and ultimately died so their children and grandchildren would not be forced to endure blatant humiliation and violence and lawful injustice because of a shallow premise. We in this generation are called upon to continue the work of our ancestors in ridding the flames of hate and bigotry and injustice in all their forms. Completing the task of securing the human rights and full equal treatment under the law for Americans of every race, gender identity, and sexual orientation will require a thorough analysis of the state of injustice and how it originated. It will require us to admit to ourselves as individuals and as a collective people the facts and realities that are often too uncomfortable to discuss. Doing so, however, will clear the path for us to make the long-needed progress that we must make together.

THE HARSH BUT URGENT CONVERSATION ABOUT RACE

The one topic that too many of us tend to avoid is the state of race relations in America. The reason for doing so is quite understandable. The grim history of racism as well as the violence and loss of human life as results of racism remain deeply disturbing and painful in remembering. There are many Americans who experienced this evil reality firsthand and remain alive to tell their stories. Thousands of individuals, both black and white, endured endless harassment and violence and lost their lives in the fight to overcome injustice and oppression. Fathers and sons, mothers and daughters, uncles and aunts, and brothers and sisters were lost over the shallow premise of racial hatred. Personally, I can understand the desire to avoid the conversation altogether and proceed with life in harmony and solidarity. However, we would only be bestowing harm upon ourselves as a country if we continue trying to overcome generational voids by pretending as if they do not exist. If the former party of Lincoln continues to pretend as if the problem of systemic injustice serves no threat to our country, we will never be able to truly unite as one nation and as one people. To continue to say, "America is not a racist country" and assume that the underlying problem consists only of "just a few bad actors" only makes one complicit in the systemic disproportionalities that affect people's daily lives.

The reality is as clear as day. Every American family must have two critical discussions with their children: teaching them right from wrong and the birds and the bees. Families of color, however, must have three conversations with their children: the difference between right and wrong, the birds and the bees, and how to endure the reality of living as a black man or black woman in

America. Families of color must teach their daughters and sons how they will be perceived and treated by many only because of their skin color. No matter how intelligent or well-articulated or how well-dressed or the choice of one's character, people of color will never be regarded by some as anything more than the negative perception that stems from the skin color itself. Some will only see the darker skin tone and associate it with a negative reality. Whether the person of color is carrying a gun or a briefcase, they will be perceived just as equally of a threat in the eyes of a racist. While anyone is capable of being the best of their self and achieving absolute greatness in life, people of color must often work ten times harder just to prove themselves worthy of achievement.

A typical argument made by many conservatives to counteract the harsh but undeniable evidence of systemic racism in the United States consists of the lack of fathers in African American households. It is true that there were indeed more fathers in the home in the African American community over half a century ago, and a child certainly has much more to gain long-term growing up in a two-parent household. Let us be reminded that instilling the values of strong character, hard work, and self-discipline into a child is not exclusive to any political party or ideology. This is a way of life that all of us as Americans take to heart and desire for our children. We desire for them to be one-hundred, ten percent of themselves in all they do in life. We desire for them to obtain an education, embark upon successful endeavors, and leave a positive mark in the world they leave behind. This profound virtue is shared by Americans in every party from every corner of society. None of this, however, erases the history and negative reality of race in this country. While there were indeed more black fathers in the household over the course of history, widespread discrimination, physical belittlement, and lynching remained a reality. Tenets of these evils remain a reality today, even as there are less fathers in African American households.

Parents should instill basic human values into their children because they desire greatness on their behalf, and it is the right thing to do. Doing so should not be done as a ploy to appease those who are racist. The only way for a person of color to appease a racist is to no longer be a person of color, which is not possible. Individuals today, whether they grow up in one-parent households and satisfy the racial stereotypes of their time or grow up in two-parent households and defy such stereotypes, will endure some sentiments of injustice in their lifetimes. Our children can achieve their hearts' desires to the fullest; as it is sometimes the long-term results of our own decisions that may hold us back in life, we cannot allow this truth to cause us to deny the reality of race and institutional bias in this country.

Growing up in a two-parent household remains no more of an escape from injustice today as it was during the height of the Jim Crow era. Are conservatives fighting on behalf of more fathers in the household because they believe in family values and want is best for children and society as a whole? Or are they just attempting to score political points by placing blame for systemic disproportionalities on people of color in an everlasting attempt to evade their responsibility in solving long, overdue challenges? The lack-of-fathers argument as well as the broken culture argument consist of nothing more than a mere distraction as well as a consistent attempt of the radical Far Right to deter from the reality of racial injustice as well as its own complicity in the state thereof.

My parents attempted to have this conversation with me many times, but there was a time in my life when I was just not interested in being part of it. I was once in complete denial concerning institutional racism and the reality of race in America. As part of me had begun to acknowledge the blatant truth, I remained in denial because I did not want to believe that something like systemic racism would even exist to begin with. Having many friends who happened to be white and part of the conservative movement also did not help me in any way to accept reality. Recent experiences, however, led me to an awakening that would lead me to not only acknowledging the existence of deeply rooted systemic injustice but dedicating my career to reversing this harsh reality for millions of Americans.

As a candidate for a seat in the Louisiana legislature in 2019, I can recall consistent conversations with many about the importance in obtaining enough white votes. The district in which I ran for office is heavily conservative and white; as a result, a significant number of black votes alone would not push me over the threshold. For many in the district, the idea of voting for a person of color to lead their district, no matter how well-educated or well-qualified they may be, is far out of the question. If I were white, the conversations about getting enough white votes would have never been required to have. There were also other well-qualified candidates of color that ran for the same office in which I did in the past but came short in achieving victory. As a candidate, however, I did receive a substantial number of white votes but nowhere near half.

An additional experience that enlightened me on the reality of race is the fact that the former principal at the high school I attended and where I subbed for seven years did not appear to be hiring any African Americans to be teachers. The only people of color working at the school were either custodians, teacher aides, substitute teachers, or secretaries. Also, when I was attempting to obtain a job as a legal assistant to an attorney in the Louisiana parish in which I lived, I can recall going into the offices of attorneys and encountered no African American staff or personnel. One may ask the question of "why would this matter so much?" It matters wholeheartedly given the history of widespread racial discrimination that generations have fought so strongly to overcome. Some employers will apply the excuse of there being no qualified African American candidates for the position in question. The simple reality of the matter is this: the only factor that made the candidate unqualified for the position was their skin color. The so-called lack of qualifications or worth has little to nothing to do with any lack of educational requirements or career experience or skills.

If I were to walk into an office building and see that most staff and personnel, if not all, consists of one race, I would question the reason for such. I would inquire upon the great lack of racial and ethnic diversity in a particular workplace. Anyone who would ignore a lack of diversity and oppose measures to promote it is complicit in the act of discriminatory practices, and I refuse to be one of those persons. The Far Right, however, would accuse me of being racist because it is disappointingly insensitive to the issue of race relations and reversing unjust practices. Those on the Far Right would assert that the only thing in which should matter is one's personal ability to perform the tasks of the job. While this is true indeed, a lack of diversity is often a huge indicator of employer bias and discrimination.

The Far Right believes that racism must be blatant for behaviors or practices of such to be considered racist. If the N word is not applied or a cross is not burning in someone's front lawn, then certain practices and behaviors are not racially offensive, or the presence of discrimination lacks thereof. For those on the Far Right, it is simply a matter of perspective. Systemic racism refers to the complex structure of systems and practices that have existed for generations. This complex structure stems from the practice of slavery that led into a century of legal discrimination and segregation, which had detrimental effects on long-term wealth and income for people of color. This structure is what causes too many to perceive people of color with negative terms simply because of their skin color. Systemic racism exists in terms of employment, health care, education, housing, law enforcement, and the legal system. It exists on a broad level. One cannot assert that it does not exist only because they have not experienced it personally, and it is far more complicated than just applying the N word or spewing blatant racial slurs. Furthermore, those who are white do not get to utter the words "what about me?" or "America is not a racist country" when it comes to building a more fair and just system for all Americans.

The unlawful murder of George Floyd at the hands of law enforcement followed by the unlawful murders of Jacob Blake and Breonna Taylor sparked deep fundamental urgency into the hearts of Americans of all races to take a bold stand against systemic racism in America. The act of doing so has never been more required upon any generation than ours. Profound disproportionalities in employment, the lack of access to greater economic and educational resources, aggressive mistreatment from law enforcement, and unfair prison sentencing demand unprecedented, razor-thin focus from leaders at every level. For too many of our leaders to pretend as if these injustices do not exist is truly disgraceful without excuse. For the Far Right to accuse those who are bold enough to call out racism and injustice of being racist themselves should be highly ashamed, and I condemn all those voices one hundred percent. For the former Vice-President, Mike Pence, to declare before the nation that systemic injustice does not exist was disgraceful.

For former President Trump to declare that he did far more for the African American community than any president since Lincoln only demonstrates and proves that he and his Far Right allies know in their minds that systemic racism exists indeed to even make this statement in the first place! Why would one who believes that systemic racism as well as the disproportionalities in employment, education, healthcare, housing, and law enforcement treatment are myths feel the need or desire to do extra for people of color to begin with? Furthermore, those who are truly anti-racist will not spend a great deal of their time attempting to prove to the world they are the least racist individuals to be met. They will not brag about how many friends of color they have or how many people of color have been in their places of residence. Instead, they will fight with everything in their power to bring about an end to racism in its entirety, and their true intentions at heart will be known through their character and sacrifices, whether they are in public office or everyday society.

I will acknowledge that there are some decent-hearted individuals who may genuinely believe that systemic racism does not exist but have yet to be educated. Anyone is capable, however, of realizing the truth concerning the state of injustice. Therefore, the need for all of us as Americans to begin talking to one another again is so great. Once we begin talking to one another, we can see each other and understand where each point of view comes from. Once we understand each other, we can reach the same path and work together to eliminate systemic racism altogether. Those who insist on name-calling and demonization and misinformation are complicit in driving us farther apart and making it ten times harder to achieve a greater reality for us all. Shame on those who insist that belittling and degrading those who disagree with them is the best way forward. There is no good reason to continue the toxic path of the previous administration. Systemic racism affects millions of lives each day, and the time is now to build a more fair and just system for every American citizen regardless of their skin color.

ELIMINATING SYSTEMIC INJUSTICE AGAINST THE LGBTQ+ COMMUNITY

The reality of race relations as well as the grave sin of systemic racism remain alive and well and thus demand swift action. However, the long-enduring fight to secure the human rights and full equal treatment under the law for every American must wholeheartedly include all of those who identify as LGBTQ+. Those who identify as gay or lesbian or as a trans-man or trans-woman are human beings who deserve no less than any of us to be treated with dignity and respect. They deserve to live in a country that honors and respects every person's right to simply exist and live under a system of laws and practices that do not punish them for existing. No human being deserves to be discriminated against by employers or insurance companies or universities or private entrepreneurs based on something so shallow such as their sexual orientation or gender identity. This should be obvious in the heart of any morally decent human being who adheres to the greatest humanly good. This is also just raw common sense. Both common sense and moral decency, however, have been compromised on the side of the Far Right.

The Far Right has always been adamantly opposed to acknowledging those in the LGBTQ+ community as fellow Americans who are no different and share no less worth as human beings. For decades, the right to marry the person you love no matter their gender had been denied in most states. Federal benefits were denied to many in same-sex marriages. Employers had the right to deny employment to gays and lesbians and trans-men and trans-women. Private entrepreneurs such as wedding planners are still able to refuse services to LGBTQ+ couples in various states. Some states even allowed health insurance companies to deny healthcare to trans-men and trans-women prior to the Affordable Care Act becoming law. For quite some time, it was illegal for gays and lesbians to serve their country in uniform. By executive order, former President Trump banned trans-men and trans-women from serving in our amazing military. He also reversed most of the civil rights protections for the LGBTQ+ community instituted by President Obama. It was President Obama who repealed the discriminatory Defense of Marriage Act and declared marriage equality as the new reality. He overturned the ridiculous Don't Ask, Don't Tell policy, and allowed every American the freedom to wear the uniform of our great military proudly without having to hide who they are. President Biden reversed the military ban on trans-men and trans-women and reinstated protections against discrimination in employment and public housing. I applaud the President wholeheartedly for standing up for human rights and equal treatment, but much work remains.

The statistics pertaining to systemic injustice against the LGBTQ+ community are heartbreaking and demands a call to our leaders to pursue bold action in reversing the wheels of injustice. According to political thinktank Center for American Progress, one in four members of the LGBTQ+ community reported encounters with some form of discrimination in 2016. According to CAP, between eleven percent and twenty-eight percent of gays and lesbians and bisexuals reported losing a promotion simply due to sexual orientation; simultaneously, twenty-seven percent of transgender workers were fired, denied employment, or rejected for a promotion simply because of their gender identity. According to CAP, 68.5 percent of those who identity as LGBTQ+ reported that discrimination at least somewhat negatively affected their psychological well-being. Discrimination against those who are LGBTQ+ has negatively impacted people's physical livelihoods and their ability to interact in their community and in our larger society. According to CAP, nearly one in three trans-men and trans-women reported experiencing harassment and to have been attacked physically. There are many gays and lesbians and even more trans-men and trans-women who have been murdered brutally simply for being who they were.

The statistics listed above demonstrate only an inkling of the deeply disturbing and heartbreaking reality of life for so many of those who identify as part of the LGBTQ+ community. They demonstrate the deep state of systemic injustice against a group of individuals who poses absolutely no harm and serves as no threat to anyone who does not identify as gay or lesbian or a trans-man or trans-woman. Far Right extremists will often cite religious liberty as justification for the mistreatment of and injustices against those who identify as LGBTQ+. It is time that we clarify the concept of religious liberty once and for all. Religious liberty is the right of every citizen to worship the deity of their choosing in a way that does not infringe upon the well-being of others. It is one's right to attend the church of their choosing and pray in public settings. It is the right to wear a shirt in public that says "May God bless you" or "As-salaam alaikum" or depicts a picture of the deity in which one worships. Religious liberty is the right to display pictures of a particular deity or scriptural verse or religious symbol on the wall or window of one's business or outside of one's property. It is the right of a child to bow their head in prayer during breakfast or lunchtime at school. It is also the right of a person to use their love for God to uplift humanity through the act of charity or ministry and to help children become morally decent human beings as they become older.

Religious liberty as a tool for growth, empathy, and compassion is something we should all hold sacred to in America. What it does not do is bestow upon any individual or business or institution the legal or moral justification to mistreat or discriminate against an individual because of their gender identity or sexual orientation. Religious liberty does not extend the right to entrepreneurs or employers or insurance companies or universities to discriminate against certain groups of Americans because of a shallow premise. It does not extend to an individual the right to harass or bully or murder someone because that person happens to be gay or lesbian or transgender. Liberty itself should apply to all Americans, and it should never be mistaken as the privilege of some to infringe upon the safety, well-being, and constitutional freedoms of others just because we disagree with who they are and how they live.

No matter how one may feel concerning scripture, they should be able to agree that no one deserves to be discriminated against or attacked physically or killed even just because of who they are and who they choose to spend their lives with. While the Bible may list certain behaviors as sin, it gives absolutely no one the right to store one sin on a pedestal while ignoring the sins of hate and injustice and greed. The Book of Matthew states for all of God's children to love one another. God calls on us to treat one another how we would want to be treated. When we choose this route, we would be fulfilling the whole law. We should store greater emphasis on condemning the immoralities that plague us collectively, rather than judging shallow matters and personal behaviors that some practice behind closed doors that do not affect others in a negative aspect.

Like most Americans, I have blood relatives who identify as part of the LGBTQ+ community. I see them no differently because of such and love them deeply. Some of my greatest friends identify as trans-men and trans-women. I would never want to see them getting mistreated or attacked in any fashion. I will fight to the death and back again for every American to live freely and safely in a democratic society. Once again, I applaud the Biden administration for reversing the inexcusable injustices enacted by former President Trump. However, there is still far to go. It is imperative that the Equality Act becomes the law of the land so that no person who identify as LGBTQ+ ever must endure legal discrimination again. There is no moral justification for anyone to be belittled and treated with less human worth just because one disagrees with someone's lifestyle or gender identity. Anyone who would discriminate against another due to sexual orientation or gender identity or race should be put out of business and certainly do not belong in positions of power representing thousands or millions of people from all walks of life. Someone who desires to serve others through leadership or entrepreneurism should serve the entire public or no one at all.

Ending systemic injustice against the LGBTQ+ community is part of a broader movement in this country to build a more fair and just system for every American citizen. Completing this task will not come easy and will be met with fierce resistance from those who stubbornly object to equality. This should only encourage us to fight a thousand times more diligently to reverse the injustices that have stood in place for far too long. It should encourage us to assume a greater role in the political arena and move us to mobilize and assert greater urgency in our leaders to get the job done. We as an American people can and must achieve this goal.

As someone who believes deeply in the right of every human to be respected and that the fate of one American is inextricably bound to the fate of us all, I will never cease to stand diligently and proudly on behalf of the LGBTQ+ community. I will defend the dignity of every citizen without shame and fight relentlessly until the day when individuals are no longer denied employment or healthcare or housing or an education simply because of who they are. I will never stop fighting until the day when individuals no longer must walk down the street in fear for their lives or safety due to the willful ignorance of unfortunately too many. I will always advocate for policies that honor the dignity of Americans from every corner of this land, and I will fight even harder until the day when shallow- and narrow-minded thinking no longer dictate the policies that impact millions of American citizens from every walk of human life. Personally, I would like to see an LGBTQ+ Million Gay/Transgender March to our nation's capital where citizens in this country join hands and lead a protest to the lights of which our nation has yet to witness on behalf of LGBTQ+ rights. Not only would such a move rock the foundation of our country, but it would also demonstrate to the world how much we truly honor the ideals of justice and equality and let everyone know that the time for bold, irreversible action is now. The time for action is NOW!

The TRUE, UNDERLYING GOAL OF "MAKE AMERICA GREAT AGAIN"

History will record the four years of Donald Trump's presidency as one of the most dark and grim eras known to what we know as America. We explored a great deal in the previous chapter into what led our democracy to the path she is on currently. It is profoundly essential to break down the truth as it is so that we know exactly what indicators in which to not neglect in the future. There was a time in America where blatant, straightforward racism and discrimination were the norms. It was completely normal to refer to blacks in public as the N word as well as other degrading terms such as "boy." Business owners could deny services to people of color without consequence or shame. Restaurants and hotels and educational facilities either had separate but poor-quality areas for people of color or turned them away altogether. People of color often endured public humiliation without valid reasoning. Interracial dating was frowned upon heavily by both races, and interracial marriage was illegal in most states.

In the late 1940s, Martin Luther King, Jr. was in love with a woman of German descent named Betty Moitz. They were deeply committed to one another and pledged to spend their lives together. Moitz was intrigued by King's lifelong desire to return to the South and eliminate racial hatred and injustice. Due to the troubling times in which they lived, King ended their relationship. King was told by his father and others that his desire to help put an end to the horrible scourge of racism in America would have been curtailed just by marriage to a white woman. Also, there were many lynchings and profound acts of police brutality against people of color. By the end of the 1950s, whites represented nearly eighty percent of our country's population. The first three quarters of the Twentieth Century were defined by Jim Crow racism that was blatant indeed and completely normal at the time. Furthermore, gays and lesbians and trans-men and trans-women knew that coming out to their families and functioning openly in society were completely out of the question. Women had little say or control and were seen widely as good for nothing more than fulfilling their "duties" in the kitchen and the bedroom.

The first three quarters of the Twentieth Century were defined by cisgender straight white-male political, economic, and cultural dominance. Any American who did not fit into this category to the fullest was deemed as less than in some fashion and often endured some form of punishment. This era would end when Americans of all races stood up for their dignity and demanded to be integrated into society fully in terms of political rights as well as economic and educational opportunities. More than anything else, they fought for equal protection in the eyes of the law. Those who marched and fought and died in the name of moral character and moral conscience changed the world forever. They erased the bigoted cultural norms that stand against all that which we as Americans would consider good and decent. As our nation surpassed into the Twenty-First Century, our society had become more diverse, inclusive, multi-racial, and multi-cultural than at any time in history. As a country, we had made great progress in race relations and were beginning to go a long way in achieving greater equality for the LGBTQ+ community. This was incredibly good news for many; for some, however, this was very displeasing.

There was a great number of people in this country who felt threatened over how diverse society had become in every fashion. Some were angry to see blacks and whites, gays and lesbians, and those who are cisgender and transgender interacting together happily without regard for shallow matters. Many were disheartened because they no longer enjoyed the privilege to control and discriminate against others without consequence. The old norms driven by cisgender straight white-male dominance were no longer considered morally acceptable. The new era of Americans embracing one another in solidarity had taken over. The election of our nation's first African American leader, Barack Obama, only furthered the anger and ignited an emboldened sense of deep-seated bitterness and hatred. After five decades of great progress on racial solidarity, followed by a new wave of immigrants to our shores, followed by the call to end systemic injustice against the LGBTQ+ community, and followed by eight glorious years of the first person of color as Commander-in-Chief, those on the Far Right finally received their greatest beacon of hope they could have ever wished for.

Donald Trump spoke directly to the hearts of those who would want nothing more than for America to return to the era where racism, xenophobia, misogyny, homophobia, and transphobia were the norms. He spoke directly to the void of those who were angry over the long-needed progress that was made and had been suppressing that void. Trump's hateful and divisive rhetoric emboldened their own hate to a place of comfort without conscience. Because the former President of the United States saw no problem in uttering racist, bigoted statements concerning people of color and immigrants publicly, many of his Far Right supporters no longer saw a need to hide their true feelings beneath the surface. Donald Trump and radical Far Right extremists want to take our country back to an era where it was acceptable to demonize and penalize those who are different than we are, and they have demonstrated openly the willingness to bring our beloved country to its knees in their quest for greater political power. Trumpism is by far the most dangerous threat to our future and to our country as we know her.

Instead of going back to a time where people who look like me or those who are gay or lesbian or transgender must fear for their lives and endure blatant injustice, I want to take us to a place where the realities of systemic injustice and hate are behind us forever. When Donald Trump and the Far Right applies the phrase "Make America Great Again," they are honestly saying "Make America White Again" and "Make America Straight and Cisgender and Xenophobic Again." It is the ideals of liberty, justice, and equal treatment that will perfect our union and continue to serve as tools for growth. During the first three quarters of the Twentieth Century, life was not bubbles and ice cream for people of color and those in the LGBTQ+ community who endured widespread discrimination and violence that often led to the loss of human life. Life was not peaches and cream for women of all races who were considered inferior to men and had no voice. So, in what fashion would we be making our nation great *again*? Who would want to return to this unpleasant time in history?

While there was a substantial number of whites who possessed not a shred of hate for anyone, there were far too many who did. Those who possessed hate and bigotry in their hearts would be the only ones that life in this era would be more than pleasant for because their ability to control and dominate served the purpose of their livelihood. The very reason this country endured nearly four centuries of slavery and a century more of Jim Crow is because someone acquired the belief in his mind that anyone and anything that is the opposite of him is inferior to him. This mere belief manifested into reality and resulted in the deaths of countless individuals. It resulted in the economic, educational, psychological, and sociological reality of systemic injustice that affect millions of Americans. I refuse to go back, and I maintain relentless faith that most Americans from all backgrounds would refuse to go back as well. We must refuse to take our country back into the era of Jim Crow.

We must follow in the steps of Dr. King and Rosa Parks and continue to move forward. Securing the human rights and full equal treatment under the law for Americans of every race and sexual orientation and gender identity is a fight we must take head on. No American's right to be treated with dignity and respect should be denied because of someone's shallow opinion. To truly uphold that right for every citizen is what will make America greater than she has ever been. In the year 2022 should none of us be arguing with or debating one another concerning someone's right to be treated fairly. No one should even possess the ability to manifest deep-seated hate and ignorance into reality. The time is now for each of us to do all that is within our power to rid this racist, xenophobic, misogynistic, homophobic, and transphobic toxic narcissistic Far Right ideology from our country once and for all.

4

A RISING GENERATION

To witness Joe Biden and Kamala Harris become president-elect and vice president-elect of the United States, respectively, bestowed a prominent sign of relief and a tremendous breath of fresh air upon millions of Americans, myself included. We were all optimistic and joyful to send a bold leader to the White House who sought to unify our beloved country and bring healing to a nation ravaged in chaos. The challenges in which had befallen us due to toxic leadership remain the greatest in decades. What we have seen is a fundamental decay in moral decency on the part of too many, which serves as a threat to us all. The tragic compromise of our moral DNA only makes it more difficult for us to conduct the business of our nation and institute sound policy solutions to the issues faced by millions of families.

Our nation now has leadership in the White House that is already delivering on the promise of unity. President Biden has pursued multiple bipartisan efforts for delivering desperately needed COVID-19 relief to the American people, which had been stalled for months under former Republican leadership in the Senate. While the President and democratic leadership on Capitol Hill were able to deliver relief to millions of families in need, it would have been pleasant to see Republicans take part in the effort. I have tremendous faith that President Biden will continue to reach across the aisle on all additional issues that affect millions of hardworking Americans both Democrat and Republican alike. The road to perfecting our union is forever enduring, and the real work begins here and now.

POLITICS MUST CONSIST OF PROBLEM-SOLVING

I will forever remember the long journey I traveled as a candidate for state representative in Louisiana's 28th District. I enjoyed the opportunity to meet thousands of honest, hardworking citizens who were desperate for change and honest, effective leadership. While I ran as a proud Democrat, I pledged to meet the concerns of citizens in both parties. I pledged to put forth a healthy balance of vision to solve the challenges faced by every citizen. All Americans are affected by issues pertaining to education, taxes, the rate of job growth, poverty, and systemic injustice. The essence of our politics exceeds party affiliation and ideological beliefs. It is the opportunity for Americans from each end of the political spectrum to put forth their ideas to increase the quality of life for both the current and subsequent generations. Deep passion on both sides, however, often prevents much needed progress.

For too long, there has been significant stagnation on critical issues that can be ignored no longer. I can assert on good authority that this is part of the reason more Americans voted in the 2020 Presidential Election than history has ever recorded. The greatest task of our generation is to fundamentally transform the United States to the lights of which history has yet to see. Our generation must stand willing and ready to complete the task of modernizing our way of life and making the system fairer and more just for every American. We must finally make the long-needed progress that has been avoided time and time again but will increase the quality of human life. Fundamentally changing our nation for the better means to complete the following tasks: providing greater pathways of economic and educational opportunities to those who lack thereof, revolutionizing our infrastructure into the Twenty-First Century, battling the threats of a changing climate and saving the future of our planet, and tackling the issues of bullying in our schools, suicide, and mental illness. All these things should come as common sense to us all, regardless of political ideology.

Our moral DNA should propel all of us as Americans to transform the goals listed above into reality because it is obviously the right move to make. The radical Far Right, however, asserts that pursuing these actions will only drive our country closer and closer to socialism. Those on the Far Right will claim that fundamentally changing our country will lead to the abandonment of the ideals of liberty and self-government when, in fact, fundamentally transforming our nation simply means to embrace the ideals that will allow us to thrive. Those on the Far Right will also claim that any effort to broaden and modernize our way of life will only make us more like Europe or ultimately something we as Americans do not recognize as normal. The irony of the matter is that this almost happened during the four years of the Trump administration through constant demonization of those who opposed the former President, separating children from their parents at the border, seeking to overturn the results of a free and democratic election, and an unprecedented attack on our Capitol that nearly sent our democracy into limbo. On November 3rd, 2021, however, eighty-one million Americans mobilized like never before and rejected the abandonment of what has defined our nation's greatness since 1776.

Any effort to establish a system that is fairer and more just is often met with one excuse after the other. Raising the minimum wage to fifteen dollars an hour so that no hardworking family is forced to live below the poverty line? Can't afford it. Revolutionizing our infrastructure by rebuilding our bridges and airports and instituting high-speed rail that will create countless new jobs right here at home? Can't afford it. Investing in clean, renewable sources of energy that will, again, create new jobs and save the future of our planet simultaneously? Can't afford it. Extending greater economic and educational opportunities and assistance to those who need them the most? Can't afford it. What

America cannot afford is to remain the wealthiest, most powerful society on Earth and refuse to provide a greater pathway to the American Dream for those who lack thereof and do the required common-sense things to increase the quality of life for every American citizen. We as Americans cannot afford to keep making the same weak and petty excuses as to why we either cannot or should not do what we all know is well within our capacity and morally required. To continue down this path would be deeply catastrophic for us all.

We must remember that it was a Republican, Ronald Reagan, who was quite conservative, who said the following: "I do not believe in a fate that will fall on us no matter what we do; I do believe in a fate that will fall on us if we do nothing." It is far beyond time that our friends in the former party of Lincoln heed the words of Reagan and lead by the examples of those who have come before them. It is time to stop developing excuse after excuse to not pursue the long overdue work that our nation is beyond capable of completing. It is time for all of us to roll up our sleeves and do the obvious without excuse to not do so.

PROVIDING GREATER PATHWAYS TO THE AMERICAN DREAM

Every American, regardless of race or family background, deserves a fair and equal shot at achieving the American Dream in its entirety. The opportunity for every citizen to climb the ladder of achievement is part of our greater essence. Any person in this country willing to sacrifice and work hard each day deserves a wage in which to support their family without slipping into poverty and despair. This is a principle that all of us should be able to agree on wholeheartedly with no problem. Data and statistics demonstrate a substantial gap between everyday hardworking Americans and those in the top one percent of income earners. They demonstrate an alarming shred of America's middle-class. In 2019, the percentage of middle-class Americans had decreased by ten percent over the previous thirty-eight years. In that same time frame, the percentage of those in high-income brackets had increased from fourteen percent to twenty percent. The percentage of low-income Americans increased from twenty-five percent to twenty-nine percent.

The last four decades saw an adequate decline in income for America's middle-class and those at or below the poverty line. At the same time, however, the top one percent saw substantial net gains that were the greatest in history. Most of this is due to decades of massive tax breaks for those at the top who can sustain without very well. It is due largely to policies that are often skewed to reward corporate interests at the expense of average workers. Some corporations will ship production overseas to avoid paying their fair share in taxes and avoid regulatory measures that provide for the safety and well-being of workers and the public. The substantial gap between those at the top and everyday common Americans can also be attributed largely to a profound lack of access to quality education, which is deeply essential in fulfilling the American Dream. The gap can be attributed also to the refusal on the part of Republican leadership to support a livable wage of fifteen dollars per hour for American workers.

As stated earlier in the chapter, we can no longer afford to remain the wealthiest, most powerful nation on the globe and deliberately continue to allow millions of Americans to wallow in the depths of despair at no fault of their own as the American Dream continues to slip away for so many. We possess all the means to eliminate the sin of income inequality and lift millions out of poverty. Once again, every effort to do so is misinterpreted often by our radical Far Right friends as efforts to turn America into a socialist country or transform us into something beyond our character. Those who lack access to economic and educational resources or are simply in need of assistance are deemed lazy and weak. Efforts to build a fairer and just system are mischaracterized as maneuvers to penalize those at the top and discourage individuals from doing for themselves. Our friends in the G.O.P. will claim that individuals should do for themselves but will chastise them for wanting to be paid a wage to support their families.

As a former candidate for office, I had the privilege of meeting thousands of poor but hardworking citizens full of pride who want nothing more than to be able to do for themselves and strived to do just that every day. My own parents worked extremely hard all their lives just so they could give my four older brothers and me a better life. My four brothers work hard each day to provide for their families. I, myself, have sacrificed day-in and day-out to achieve the greater things in life. Most of us, however, will require assistance at times. Ordinary common folks who work hard and sacrifice without shame to give their children the greater things in life do not appreciate being called lazy or freeloaders who only desire a handout, and I heavily condemn those who would chastise millions of genuine-hearted folks just for wanting a livable wage or assistance during a crisis. This profoundly out-of-touch and narrow-minded demonization must come to an end; providing greater pathways to the American Dream for every citizen should be the priority. It is the right and moral thing to do. There is no probable excuse to continue providing lucrative tax breaks to millionaires and billionaires at the expense of investing in education and revolutionizing our crumbling infrastructure and extending aid to families and children in need.

There is no excuse as to why countries such as Denmark and Norway can provide a livable wage in lieu of other needed services to their citizens while the wealthiest nation on Earth provides excuses to not do the same. We can live up to our moral DNA and stop punishing everyday folks who have done nothing to deserve punishment. We can ensure that there is a regulatory system in place to protect workers as well as consumers from abuse and unethical practices. We can ensure that every child in America has access to a world-class education that will take them as far as they are willing to go. We can also ensure that college students are not knee-deep in debt for achieving the one thing that should be an absolute right for every child upon birth. Just as we have Social Security and health savings accounts, we should institute what should be known as higher ed savings accounts to make it easier for families to save for their children's college tuitions. We should also make two-year community colleges free of charge. There are many Americans who desperately desire to achieve a college education but cannot afford to do so. They should be able to do better for themselves without having to not be able to at no fault of their own.

We should also expand access to trade schools, particularly in rural areas, because a great number of children who grow up in rural communities may not work so well with numbers or science but are quite good with their hands and know how to build things and operate machinery. These children deserve just as much as students at Harvard and Yale to ascend as far as their talents and abilities will ascend them. Transforming these goals into a reality is very well within our capacity. My message to our Republican friends is quite simple: come on board with the changing times and let us do together what we all know is right on behalf of the American people. Let us secure our economic future with boundless opportunities for those who lack thereof. If you cannot join your fellow Americans in an expanding nation in changing times, then simply get out of the way and stop blocking much-needed progress that will harness a new reality for our country that will secure a legacy of greatness for our posterity.

COMBATTING THE THREATS OF CLIMATE CHANGE

One of the greatest challenges of our time consists of the threats put forth by a warming climate. Dealing with climate change requires each of us as Americans to do our part and be honest about the unfortunate reality that has befallen us. It will require our elected officials to provide the bold leadership we so desperately need and enact the standards and rules for a healthy environment. We need to transition from the production of oil to establishing industries producing alternative sources of energy that will be safer for our planet. There should be greater emphasis on clean energy, solar and wind power, and electricity. While transitioning to safer methods of producing and operating energy will be safer for the longevity of the earth, doing so will also create millions of jobs. For anyone to dismiss the long-term threats of a warming climate as mythical or not regard the threats with great urgency is selfish and displeasing. It demonstrates a profound disregard for science and facts as well as a significant disregard for our common humanity and generations to come later.

The facts concerning climate change are as clear as day and should be alarming to us all. Over the last century, the temperature of the Earth has seen an increase of one degrees Fahrenheit. Since 1880, our oceans have risen approximately eight to nine inches. Much of this increase had taken place just over the past several decades. The cause for the oceans' rise consists of rising global temperatures, which results in melting ice caps. It is projected that sea levels along United States coastlines will rise approximately one foot by the year 2050. Rising temperatures are the result of an eroding ozone layer in the atmosphere, which is solely responsible for omitting dangerous radiation from the sun. The issue of climate change constitutes a critical matter of life and death. While our generation and the next few generations may not feel the immediate consequences, there will come the generation that will be affected drastically if we do not act now.

If we do not begin as of this moment listening to science as well as our individual and collective moral conscience and choose to pursue the tough decisions, there will come a day when major cities such as New York and Los Angeles and Miami will be under water. If we do not begin the process right now, there will come a time when the air in which we breathe will not be suitable for human lungs. Life as we know it will cease to exist with little to no chance of recourse. Many of our Republican allies, unfortunately, will only continue to dismiss the long-term threats of global warming as fiction and a trojan horse for higher taxes and greater government infringement upon our personal liberties. They will continue to make these same arguments again and again even as the obvious facts and recent research have indicated the grave threats to us all.

What more will it take for our friends in the Republican Party to acknowledge some of the unfortunate realities of the world in which we live? What will it take for the radical Far Right to get on board and meet the threats to our generation as well as our children and grandchildren and so on? Refusing to make the uncomfortable transition to meet the threats of climate change or any other fundamental threat to our humanity just because doing so may be inconvenient and require a little extra work and sacrifice on the part of some only demonstrates profound laziness and, once again, an utter disregard to help others.

Addressing a warming climate should not be a matter of anyone's opinion or personal feelings. It should not be a matter of politics. It should be a matter of solving problems. All our political leaders have a moral responsibility to take the necessary steps to meet the threats before us. They are required morally to set proper standards for full efficiency and invest in clean and renewable sources of energy. President Biden's decision to halt oil production as well as the development of the Keystone Pipeline, which was dangerous and threatening to indigenous communities, was best for our country. He provided bold leadership by returning our nation to the Paris Accord Agreement; this acknowledges that meeting the threats of climate change is a global responsibility.

There is much more work to be done. I have abounding faith in our ability as Americans to overcome any threat or crisis when we choose to listen to our conscience and do what we know is morally just. This defines the core of our national character. It defines our fortitude and ability to persevere in the most discouraging times. Preserving the long-term health of our planet will not come easy, but it must be a fundamental priority. We can overcome this threat by doing what we do best in America, which is moving forward even when we are uncertain. We can choose to put our humanity first and give our posterity a planet in which is safe and stable. Let us make it happen.

TACKLING BULLYING, SUICIDE, AND MENTAL ILLNESS IN AMERICA

Three issues that are seldomly discussed on the political front consist of bullying in our schools, suicide, and treating mental illness. These are issues that affect millions of lives each day. It is imperative that leaders at every level begin to address them fully. It is also critical to break down each issue, demonstrate how each of them relate, and how the issues affect the population. Once we become better familiarized and enlightened with bullying and suicide and mental illness, our country will be in a greater position moving forward.

The act of bullying is a major problem that countless children endure every day in our schools. It has major ramifications on a child's ability to obtain their education as well as a child's self-confidence and overall view of self. Bullying can lead a child to question their measure of self-worth and accept a false reality rooted in emotional trauma, which is often the result of negative treatment from others. As someone who was bullied in school an adequate number of times, I know firsthand the tormented suffering that can occur from the act of bullying. As a former educator for seven years, I have witnessed other students being bullied and held their bullies accountable. Upon becoming a motivational speaker, I met an amazing student named John Jarrow who took his own life after suffering through years of bullying. I knew him to be one of the most kind and respectful kids one could have ever had the pleasure of meeting. There are many kids like John who have followed in the footsteps of harassment and torture and felt as if they could continue with life no longer.

As a motivational speaker, I have spoken to and counseled many students who were victims of bullying. As an educator for seven years, I have always taken the issue of bullying with extreme urgency and told all my students to never be afraid to speak up and come to me if they are being harassed or mistreated by others. This is an issue that will always have a deep place in my heart. For some of us, bullying can constitute many different scenarios. If we intend to improve the lives of millions of children across our country, there must be a definitive description of bullying itself and specific acts thereof. Bullying should be defined as the physical, verbal, mental, and/or emotional belittlement from one person to another. Specific acts should include name-calling, chastising, threats of violence, pushing, punching, kicking, and physical mocking. Bullying occurs when one individual exalts physical or mental power over others.

According to several sources, approximately twenty percent of students across America ages 12-18 experienced acts of bullying. The same sources indicate that most bullies possessed the ability to influence students' perception of others, had greater social standing, were physically stronger or larger, and came from families in higher income brackets. A great deal of children and young adults are also being harassed and bullied on social media. Sources indicate a strong correlation between bullying and suicidal thoughts. One source also indicates that an individual can endure up to forty years of clinical depression that is the result of childhood bullying. Sometimes this deep depression leads to suicide. The facts are clear as day.

No matter what form in which bullying manifests, it is evil and should not be tolerated under any circumstances. Under no circumstance should a child be subjugated to acts of harassment and emotional torture. Every child and adolescent deserve a safe and secure environment in which to obtain their education and interact with their friends on social media without being at the mercy of evil. What is more unfortunate than bullying itself is when those in which we entrust to watch over our children during school hours take the issue lightly.

Each of us share a moral obligation to protect and defend every child with all that is in our power. Therefore, it is time to enact an anti-bullying law at the federal level.

A new federal law should require all schools to tackle down greater than ever to put an end to bullying in all its manifestations and discipline every student who commit acts of bullying. This should also require school districts to issue fines ranging from fifty to one-hundred dollars to the parents of those who commit acts of bullying because the behavior is acquired in the home. A new federal law should also hold a bully accountable by law if it is determined that a suicide is the result of bullying from the bully in question. This law should allow the families of those whose children committed suicide to be compensated by the local school board. There is absolutely no excuse in which to not pursue this ambitious effort to protect our kids. I call on our nation's leaders to make this federal law a reality immediately. I call also on the great people of this country to write your congresspersons and senators, urging them to do the same. Let us get the job done.

As stated earlier in the chapter, acts of bullying often lead some to mental illness. Mental illness in this country is an additional issue for which plagues the lives of too many Americans. In addition to bullying, many manifestations of mental illness are the result of chemical imbalance in the brain, which becomes only a hundred times worse when combined with emotional trauma. This crisis exists at no fault of the individual who is suffering. One statistic indicates that approximately 51.5 million Americans suffer from some form of mental illness. According to the Anxiety and Depression Association of America (ADAA), clinical anxiety disorders are among the most common manifestations of mental illness in the United States. Depression is also widespread in our country. Over seventeen million Americans suffer from clinical depressive disorder.

The state of suffering in mental disarray differs from person to person. While there are some who can maintain a sense of stability to an adequate degree, there are others who will slip into addictions to alcohol or opioids. There are some who will resort to breaking the law or other extreme behaviors that result sometimes in violence or death. Some may shoot up a school or movie theater, while others exhibit behaviors that destroy families and wreck communities. Some of those suffering from mental illness will zone themselves out from the rest in the world in consistent void and agony. All of this has a profoundly negative impact on the lives of individuals and our country entirely. Drug abuse and alcohol addiction, which often stem from deeply rooted trauma, both lead to acts of violence and death. They also lead to physical illnesses such as heart disease, diabetes, kidney failure, and erosion of the liver.

The time is now for our nation's leaders to take bold steps in reversing the scourge of mental illness in America. We must devote all resources necessary to increase access to mental health treatment so that those in need of help have a place to turn. I wholeheartedly support President Biden's proposal for a public health care option for those who lack health insurance, which is often the reason many do not seek treatment. Those suffering from severe depression and anxiety deserve an opportunity to overcome their trauma and experience the greater gifts that life has to offer. They deserve a chance to live in peace among those who love them. To every American suffering from some form of mental illness or trauma that is deeply rooted, to everyone who suffers from alcohol or drug addiction to every person struggling day to day just to keep a smile on your face to shield your pain, and to every individual who feels as if you are worthless and that you would rather be dead, know that you are somebody. You are a beautiful child of God who can overcome all your pain and rise to whatever level of peace and happiness you wish. Treating mental illness and storing the mental void of all those suffering behind them forever is a priority we must set right now.

THE HOPE OF A NEW GENERATION

Our generation stands at a major crossroads. We have an opportunity to fulfill the initiatives to increase the quality of life for every American and pass on a greater, more perfected union to our posterity. We can make the investments that will harness long-term stability that will reach Americans from every corner of this proud land.

We can pursue the cautionary measures to preserve the longevity of our planet and create new industries that will foster growth and innovation. We can also do everything in our power to protect our children and hold accountable those who would inflict harm upon them. We can provide support and assistance to the most vulnerable and bring them up to par with the rest of us. The only way we can accomplish these vital tasks is through mobilizing and supporting candidates at every level of government who will pledge to get the job done.

The time for excuses and partisan division must come to an end. The time is now to stop developing excuse after excuse to continue giving billions in tax breaks to the top one percent and to other countries, while finding every possible excuse to not aid Americans who need it the most. The time is now for we as Americans to re-apply our moral DNA like never before and be the absolute best of ourselves personally and to each other. If we in this generation answer the call of fate and be the country that we know how to be, our children tomorrow will recall what we did today and say proudly, "the hope of a new generation is now a reality!"

Part II: ADDITIONAL ISSUES (SPEECHES)

5

HER BODY, HER CHOICE, HER FREEDOM

Enormous challenges face the current generation of Americans. Some of these challenges include jobs that often do not pay well enough to support a family, lack of access to quality education, lack of access to adequate healthcare, poverty, systemic injustice, and climate change. Solving these challenges will require common purpose and razor-thin focus from those of whom we elect to serve our nation. The challenges in which I just mentioned truly are not as complicated as some would portray them to be. Ensuring that every American worker is paid a livable wage to support their family and prevent them from sliding into poverty at no fault of their own should come as common sense to any person. Affording every child access to an education that will take them as far as their dreams will take them should be something that Democrats, Republicans, liberals, and conservatives should be able to agree on wholeheartedly. Expanding access to healthcare is something that no educated or common sense-minded individual should be opposed to. The voices that are opposed to ending laws and practices that discriminate against individuals because of who they are and how they look should just simply be ignored. Finally, combatting the threats to an alarmingly warming climate should invoke deep urgency into the hearts of all individuals to do all that is required to preserve the longevity of our planet.

All the issues I just mentioned should unite Americans from every political background with the goal of making the quality of life just a little bit easier for all citizens. There is one issue, however, that involves much greater complication and requires an open-minded from all sides to reach a conclusion that meets the needs of those affected. The issue in which I am referring to is that of abortion. This is an issue that stirs deep passion and conviction among those who proclaim to be either pro-life or pro-choice. Those who refer to themselves as either pro-choice or pro-life crosses over into both political parties and may possess a different foundation for their perspective on the issue. For decades, Americans have debated, marched in the streets, and argued in the courts, advocating diligently on behalf of their perspective. No matter the perspective, however, the greatest starting point to reaching common ground and establishing an end to a longstanding stalemate will require greater insight, communication, and unbiased self-reflection into the issue.

For a decade, I considered myself to be what one would refer to as pro-life. I was someone who would tell others that abortion was murder and needed to be abolished in its entirety. I was someone who would proclaim that Planned Parenthood and other institutions that provide abortions needed to be defunded. I would even assert that there was an effort among pro-choice elected officials to assert greater emphasis on women of color to obtain abortions. For quite some time, I was an individual who adhered to this kind of thinking and believed with all my heart that it was the best way forward. While I possessed the greatest of intentions, I failed to consider the greater reality concerning the issue of abortion and how it affects millions of women and the nation altogether.

During the 2020 presidential election, I can remember driving through town and seeing countless signs on the sides of roads encouraging citizens to vote YES for an amendment to add "life begins at conception" to the Louisiana state constitution. Days before the election, I would dismiss the signs and plan to vote yes by default. On Election Day, however, I stood behind the voting booth thinking deeply on this issue. After ten minutes of deep, unbiased soul-searching, not only did I vote NO, I reached the conclusion stating that abortion is far more complicated than just resorting to personal feelings. I realized that ending the stalemate and solving the problem will require a greater understanding of the issue in its entirety and how certain policy solutions affect the country long-term. I also realized that male politicians surrounded by their mantrum walls of wealth and privilege who have no understanding of struggle or any reality beyond their own are the very last people who should be making personal health decisions for women and their well-being. At that moment, I went from what one would portray falsely as "pro-life" to someone who believes that women should maintain autonomy over their personal health and decisions that affect them personally and that do not affect others negatively. Not only am I one-hundred percent pro-choice and supportive of women's voices and respect in society, but I will also fight to the death to combat all attempts to curb women's reproductive rights as well as all attempts to overturn Roe v. Wade.

One of the persons I think of concerning this deeply complicated and personal issue is my godmother. Lisa Allen was one of millions of women who received an abortion in her lifetime. Lisa was my speech therapist in both fifth and sixth grade, and I overcame the habit of stuttering much greatly due to her. We would become very close over time. We shared countless conversations that I remember to this very day, and I will never forget the wisdom and life lessons she taught me. Not only was she my godmother, but she was also my friend. While she is now deceased, Lisa is one of the greatest women and individuals I have ever met in my life, and I miss her every day. There are still many days when I become teary-eyed and will cry even because I love her with all my heart and miss her so much. When I hear others refer to women who receive an abortion as baby killers or murderers, I am deeply hurt and offended because I think of Lisa.

There are millions across America just like Lisa who are the kindest at heart and want nothing more than a life of harmony for themselves and others. None of these women deserve to be demonized and chastised due to the willful ignorance and failure on the part of some to see the larger picture. The act of murder or inflicting harm upon their offspring is the very last intention on the part of women who are struggling and simply desire to pursue their constitutional rights and live out their lives without imposing harm or evil upon anyone else. Those who would bestow judgment upon those who believe differently from them on this heartfelt issue only make it far more difficult to reach common ground and do what needs to be done on behalf of us all. Complicated issues such as that of abortion covers a prominent grey area, and sometimes we must look beyond our own heart and way of thinking to achieve progress. Americans from every end of the political spectrum have something to offer to the table, but judgment, belittlement, and demonization should not be included on the menu.

There are those who truly believe that abortion is murder and support efforts to strip women of autonomy over their bodies and their personal health. These individuals believe that curbing access to receive an abortion will lower the number of abortions and end the process altogether. There are some, as stated before, who will chastise women who receive abortions as well as those who are open-minded to the issue. Personally, I have lost quite a few friends due to reaching a greater enlightened understanding of abortion as well as other issues. The reality for me is this: I may lose my best friend, I may lose all my friends, but I will not lose America. None of us must sacrifice losing all that makes our nation exceptional. States such as Louisiana, Texas, and Mississippi have instituted laws restricting access to abortion. The greatest tragedy is instituting these policies due to personal feelings based on a limited scope of reality rather than facts and the broader reality. It is a moral tragedy to please a certain aspect of the electorate for mere political gain while refusing to consider how certain policies would affect an entire population.

I challenge leaders in all fifty states to please listen to their constituents and reach across the aisle before instituting policies that are doomed to bestow harm and evil upon the lives of too many. I implore all those who proclaim to be pro-life to consider the larger aspect of the issue and not refer to those who are pro-choice as evil or murderers or non-Christian. Would it be in the interest of Christ and the betterment of humanity if we restrict access to legal abortions that are safe and secure rather than surrendering women to methods are not only unsafe but dangerous for both the mother and the fetus? Would Christ judge someone by calling her a murderer or baby killer or would He seek a greater understanding of her as a person as well as her circumstances?

Is it morally sound to store enormous emphasis on the beauty and importance of an unborn child and why they should not be aborted but totally disregard their well-being once entered the world? Is it morally just to deny the child's healthcare and educational needs as well as the mom's ability to afford the child the basic things they need while growing up? Do not restrict a woman's access to a safe and legal abortion on religious grounds while opposing the initiatives to increase the quality of life for the child once they are born. Do not deny a livable wage to the child's parents, making it only more difficult for them to keep a roof over the child's head and put food on the table and clothes on the child's back. Do not prejudge a woman's circumstances based on a narrow scope of reality, which will only make life more difficult and does not solve the greater problem in question. While we are at it, the time is now to end the assault on women in this country and put an end to the toxic masculine standards that only seek to control and demonize and drown out the voices and concerns of women and their needs and overall reality.

One of the greatest principles of our nation's founding was individual liberty. Liberty is what allows every individual to work hard for their greatest dreams and highest aspirations without limit. It is what allows individuals to be free and in control of their own destiny as long as no one imposes upon the well-being of others. The fires that have flamed the torches of liberty for nearly three centuries still burn to this day. Every subsequent generation of Americans is responsible for keeping the flame going. The glorious victory of the American Revolution, the ratification of our constitution, the signing of the Emancipation Proclamation, and the success and continuity of Roe

v. Wade have guarded the torches of liberty for so long. Let us not relent now. Let us stop being conservatives and liberals and do what is in the best interests of our posterity. Let us proceed beyond what many would consider pro-life and pro-choice and do all that needs to be done to increase the quality of life for children already here and truly reach common ground on the issue of abortion without judgment or demonization from either side.

Let us not forget the sacrifices in which established and prolonged the nation in which we live. Let us never stop marching, protesting, and working on behalf of what protects and what makes us who we are as Americans. When a woman makes the conscientious but enormously difficult decision to get an abortion, it is just that. It is a decision. It is her body; it is her choice; it is her freedom. This freedom is both granted and protected by the constitution of the United States. It is about time that some of us stop applying the constitution only when it is politically convenient and apply it in every aspect of American life. Liberty is our greatest principle, but once liberty becomes a tool for some to control and demonize others based on a closed-minded reality, it has just gone from the God-given gift of liberty to the man-made curse of tyranny. We the American people are better than that, and it is beyond time that some of us begin to live up to our greater character just somewhat better.

6

GUNS DO KILL PEOPLE

America will never forget the deadly mass shooting that occurred at Sandy Hook Elementary School in Newtown, Connecticut on December 14th, 2012. It is the fourth deadliest mass shooting that has occurred in the United States since 1949. Twenty-seven individuals, consisting of mostly small children between the ages of six and seven years old, lost their lives. Multiple adult staff members were gunned down as well. The perpetrator who was responsible killed his mom prior to driving to Sandy Hook and initiating a deadly act of violence. He killed himself as law enforcement and first responders arrived at the school.

I can still remember the pain I felt just thinking in my mind of the small children being shot at by a military-style machine gun in an act of rage. I can still recall as clear as day the moment at the diner when all I could do is lay my head down in disarray. As an uncle of nieces and nephews and a former educator at both the elementary and secondary levels, I could only ask myself of whom would desire to inflict death or harm upon innocent children who would never hurt anyone. I was speaking at my old high school on the very day of the Sandy Hook shooting. While I was speaking words of life into children in one place, I had no idea that the lives of children in another place far away were being taken away. It was this act of violence that sparked fundamental passion into my heart on the issue of gun violence. What was even more disheartening than the initial act of violence was witnessing our nation's leaders in Congress take no action to keep guns out of the hands of those who would impose harm.

In addition to the violence in Newtown, there were more mass shootings that resulted in countless deaths. The 2012 mass shooting that occurred at a Century 16 movie theater in Aurora, Colorado resulted in the deaths of twelve individuals as well as the injuries of seventy others. Let us not forget the second most deadly mass shooting in the United States since 1949, which consists of the 2016 shooting that occurred at an Orlando nightclub. Forty-nine individuals lost their lives during this incident, leaving fifty-eight injured. The primary weapon of choice was indeed a semi-automatic assault rifle. All the deaths and fifty-eight of the injuries were the result of gunfire. One of the weapons used in the shooting was tear gas. Thirty-five of the one-hundred, forty-two mass shootings that have occurred in the United States were committed with semi-automatic rifles, while sixty-eight of the shootings were committed with semi-automatic handguns. Furthermore, high-capacity magazines were used in approximately half of all mass shootings. Semi-automatic rifles were applied in six of the ten deadliest mass shooting events throughout the country. These are only a small number of events that have occurred that resulted in tragedy; there are countless more incidents where innocent individuals died at the hands of gun violence.

There is absolutely no doubt that gun violence is one of the greatest challenges facing our nation. It remains a serious threat to innocent lives everywhere at any given point. Not only does the act of gun violence result in great tragedy, but it also bestows great pain and loss into the hearts of many. Those of whom will suffer the most are moms and dads, sisters and brothers, uncles and aunts, grandmothers and grandfathers, and very close friends who are often regarded as family themselves. Much of the loss of life that occurs throughout our country, in addition to the anger and heartbreak that follow, can very well be prevented. The tendency of our elected officials to stand idly by and do either very little or absolutely nothing must come to an end. Furthermore, simply responding to every course of action to solve the issue of gun violence with the same old excuse of "guns don't kill people; people kill people" must also come to an end.

If we are to truly curb the occurrence of gun violence and save countless lives, we must sit aside personal feelings and assess the facts and reality concerning gun violence and how certain policies stand to affect it. The fact of the matter is that personal feelings do not solve problems because they too often ignore the unfortunate reality that so many of us are not ready to confront. Facing the unfortunate reality of gun violence and taking it head-on is first place in eliminating the problem. Voices responding to every effort to provide greater safety standards in society as mere attempts to curtail the Second Amendment and confiscate people's guns are rooted not in reality but misinformation and fear. The spread of misinformation and fear on gun violence are rooted in a limited scope of the broader issue. Those who would rather sit back and do nothing on this serious issue are complicit in every loss of life and infliction of injury that occur in mass shootings as well as other acts of gun violence.

Simply stating that someone can inflict death or harm using other methods besides guns is completely irrelevant to the conversation at hand. All those who were gunned down in a rapid pace or from far away or through an additional surface were often killed with guns, particularly semi-automatic assault rifles. Those killed in Aurora and Orlando and the children killed in Newtown were gunned down with semi-automatic machine guns that should have never been for sale to begin with. If we do not assess the facts and the unfortunate reality behind gun violence and continue with the same decade-old excuses as to why we should not pursue action, countless more lives will be lost in vain, many more will endure injuries that are often permanent, and many more hearts and lives will be broken.

Let us be very clear about one critical element concerning the issue at hand. We must understand that no move to curb gun violence is a disguised attempt to abolish the Second Amendment and take away the guns of law-abiding citizens. It is no attempt to make it more difficult for law-abiding individuals to protect themselves from possible harm. It is also no attempt to transform society into a police-state. The voices repeating these absurd and untrue assertions are only fearmongering and making it only more difficult to achieve progress.

It is a fact that the reality of guns for hunters in rural towns such as Moreauville, Louisiana, where I once lived, differs completely from that of those battling street violence in cities such as my hometown, Chicago, Illinois. Furthermore, law-abiding citizens who own firearms to either go hunting and/or protect themselves and their families should never be included in the same category as those who would obtain a firearm for the mere purpose of pursuing violence. The questions going forward consists of the following: what is the best course of action we as a country must take to ensure protection of the Second Amendment while keeping guns, whether they are handguns or semi-automatic assault rifles, out of the hands of those who would impose harm on the innocent? How we the American people can fulfill this goal as we seek to protect future generations from deadly acts of violence?

As our nation proceeds forward in the quest to fundamentally curb gun violence, we must examine some of the important facts concerning gun laws and their effects on the population. For so long, there has been the long-asserted notion that greater gun control leads to greater violence. However, certain laws passed in various states concerning gun ownership speaks differently. The state of California, for example, has the strictest gun laws in the entire country. Some of the laws include a statewide recording of all firearms as well as a ten-day waiting period. In addition to background checks, the sale of semi-automatic assault rifles is not permitted. The state does not recognize concealed carry permits issued by other states, and non-residents cannot obtain a permit in California. These laws are strictly enforced by both the state and local municipalities. Similar laws exist in states such as my home state of Illinois, New York, Rhode Island, Massachusetts, Maryland, and New Jersey. Some of these states require individuals to undergo training before being permitted to purchase a firearm. In Massachusetts, individuals must obtain a permit from their local police precinct. The process involves paperwork, an interview, and a background check.

All the states I just mentioned not only have the lowest percentage of gun ownership but the lowest rates of deaths due to gun violence. Rhode Island has the lowest gun death rate, which consists of approximately three deaths per one-hundred thousand individuals. This is followed by the state of Massachusetts, which has the second lowest rate of gun violence in the country. California, Illinois, New York, Maryland, and New Jersey follow behind Rhode Island and Massachusetts with the lowest rates of gun deaths per capita. To the contrary, the states with the least strict gun laws have the highest rates of gun violence. Some of the states with the most lenient gun laws include Mississippi, Texas, Alaska, Louisiana, and Georgia. The state of Mississippi, for example, has the highest number of gun deaths per capita, which consists of over twenty-two individuals per capita. The other states mentioned are not very far behind. Texas, for example, has no laws regarding the purchase of firearms regardless of age. This means that any person, regardless of criminal background or mental capacity or potential danger posed to society, can legally purchase a firearm. Over thirty-five hundred deaths occurred in Texas in 2017 at the hands of gun violence: this consists of 12.4 deaths per capita. This number increased to three-thousand, six-hundred eighty-three deaths in 2021. This was higher than the number of gun deaths in California, which has a much higher population than Texas, with gun deaths totaling two-thousand, eight-hundred seventy-two.

These are just some of the important facts and statistics concerning the reality of gun violence in America. Every number or percentage mentioned represents a life that was taken. It represents a life that was full of potential, and, more importantly, it represents a human being who was loved deeply by family and friends. The lives of countless women, children, the elderly, and basic family men have been lost. Those who have died at the hands of gun violence could very well still be alive. They could still be enjoying life with their children and spouses and families who loved them deeply. They could still be contributing to the aspects of a more perfect world in which for all of God's children to live. How many lives must be taken before we choose to do the right thing? How many more children and young adults must die before our leaders decide to stop putting political expedience before the safety and well-being of the citizens they serve? How many more excuses will be made before each of us decide that the time is now to put aside personal feelings regarding gun control and do what must be done in the best interest of moral conscience and the safety of every American citizen?

The time has come to abandon the same excuses that have been made time and time again as to why we should not enact laws that will protect the innocent by keeping guns out of the hands of those who pose a potential threat to society. The time has come for those in Washington to enact universal background checks, ensure that those who purchase a firearm are mentally capable of handling one, prohibit the sale of firearms at the gun range, require all individuals to be permitted and licensed to own a firearm, and, more important than ever, ban the sale of semi-automatic assault rifles that have historically inflicted far more harm than good. There is not any good reason to not enact the commonsense laws to protect the innocent from those who would impose a danger to them. There is no good reason to continue applying personal feelings or ignorant thinking to a crisis that is complicated beyond measure and demands bold action. To the leaders in Washington: you were not elected to sit back and do nothing. You were not elected to invoke opposition at every turn, storing your own political interests ahead of the safety and security of those who elected you. To the governors making it easier for those who would impose harm to purchase a firearm: shame on you. Shame on you for putting the lives of the public in their most vulnerable state just to give yourselves a more positive image in the eyes of your constituencies.

If we do not enact reasonable gun control that keeps guns out of reach of criminals, more lives will be lost, and the violence will only continue from there. We as a nation can change that. We can redefine an unfortunate reality that is based on lies and misinformation and tragedy and loss into one of security and safety, promise and hope, discernment and conscience, and opportunity and progress. The only thing that would stand to prevent us from moving forward is our own refusal to do so. The America I know is one that rises above every level of apprehension and achieves her reach for the stars no matter the circumstances that lie ahead. Let us be the generation that harnesses this new reality and erases the fear and false narratives concerning guns and the violence in which follows that some would have us to believe for their own selfish reasons. Once we do that, we will truly live up to our Preamble of ensuring Domestic Tranquility and continue to make America a more perfect union.

7

THE ROARING LION OF WHITE SUPREMACY

The issue of race relations in this country holds deep conviction and passion in the hearts of individuals from every walk of life. The murder of George Floyd at the hands of disgraced former police officer Derek Chauvin on May 25th, 2020 sparked fundamental urgency upon Americans of every race and every kind to pursue bold action. Millions of Americans marched and protested in the streets in the name of justice and equal treatment. As the nation watched while former Officer Chauvin kneeled on Mr. Floyd's neck for thirty minutes, disabling him from breathing, we knew that enough was enough. We knew that the consistent, disproportionate mistreatment of people of color at the hands of law enforcement had gone too far, and the long overdue work to abolish injustice must begin. Followed by the additional deaths of Breonna Taylor, Jacob Blake, and Daunte Wright as well as the riots that had taken place as a result, history will record this era as the greatest moment of civil unrest and racial division since the 1960s.

The work of establishing full equal treatment under the law for every citizen will be long and forever enduring. Abolishing the unjust laws and unfair practices that plague the lives of those who are non-white will not be met easily and, unfortunately, will garner fierce opposition from those who remain insensitive to any reality beyond their own limited scope of the world we live in. We all know that laws and practices that discriminate against others persist in the areas of law enforcement, employment, education, and healthcare. The injustices that plague the lives of Americans exist not only in terms of race and skin tone but also in terms of sexual orientation and gender identity. If America is to truly bring about an end to these injustices and establish a society where all of God's children can function together in peace and solidarity, we can no longer sugarcoat or ignore the longstanding root of the hate that has led to centuries of psychological agony and countless deaths. We must acknowledge that the hate that has plagued the lives of people of color, women of all kinds, and the LGBTQ+ community alike consists of fruits of the same poisonous tree, which is none other than white supremacy.

There are many who may describe racism or white supremacy as merely the disliking at heart of another race or kind. Dictionaries will often describe white supremacy as merely the feeling of racial superiority among whites to all other races as well as the inferiority of people of color, Jews, Catholics, and members of the LGBTQ+ community. In one aspect, both perspectives are correct. There was once a time when an individual felt as if his kind was superior to all those who were not like him. As history unfolded, this mere feeling of racial, cultural, and moral superiority would be manifested into reality and lead to four centuries of slavery and physical bondage. This would be followed by an additional century of Jim Crow injustice. Countless individuals were beaten and killed while standing in line to vote, while others would lose their right to vote altogether. There would be separate restroom facilities, restaurants, sitting areas, and other public venues for blacks and whites. During the Jim Crow era, approximately four thousand-forty-three Americans, both black and white, were lynched from trees. Many more Americans of every race and ethnicity would go on to endure brutal attacks and blatant discrimination in the name of hate and white supremacy.

In assessing the evil sin of hate and the negative consequences it has bestowed upon race relations in our nation, the resulting impact upon the Asian-American community cannot be ignored. History will record the COVID-19 pandemic as one of the deadliest crises ever befallen upon not just the United States but the entire world. While it brought about the deaths of well over seven-hundred thousand American lives and millions worldwide, leaving countless families reeling in agony, there were greater far-reaching consequences that exceeded the initial pandemic itself. Due to the pandemic's origin, there was growing negative sentiment on the part of some directed at Americans of Asian descent. According to statistics gathered by the FBI, the number of hate crimes targeting Asian-Americans increased seventy percent in 2020 in contrast to the previous year. According to the advocacy group Stop AAPI Hate, there were over two-thousand, eight hundred hate incidents directed at Asian-Americans throughout the country in the year 2020. Incidents involving attacks on the AAPI community include those that were both verbal and physical. There were also greater incidents of workplace discrimination, refusal of service, and public humiliation. Many of those attacked included women, children, and the elderly.

What was deeply unfortunate and worse than the initial rise in hate crimes was the consistent tendency of disgraced former President Donald Trump to feed into the rising negative sentiment on the part of some towards the AAPI community. Through his consistent downplaying of the pandemic and constant use of the xenophobic terms "China virus" and "kung flu," former President Trump spoke directly to the void and ignorance that too many felt regarding Asian Americans and Pacific Islanders. Even as the number of hate crimes continued to rise, he would continue to feed into the negative sentiment towards Americans of Asian descent. Tapping into people's fears and that with which is the worst in the hearts of so many was the fundamental political strategy of the disgraced former President, which consists of the reason for the recent rising sentiments of racism and xenophobia on the part of his supporters. Instead of using this dire moment of crisis to unite our country based on who we are and chart a course going forward based on hope and progress, Mr. Trump used one of our darkest hours to arouse his political base by torching the flames of white supremacy and dividing the American people farther apart. This was exactly what he did in the face of racial unrest on countless other occasions simply because this is what Donald Trump does best. While President Biden signed into law protections for the AAPI community due to rising hate, there is still far to travel as we seek to carve out racial disparities and heal the wounds of racial animosity and division.

Over recent decades, the wrath of white supremacy has come down hard on those who align within the LGBTQ+ community. There was a time in this country when coming out of the closet and functioning normally within society was far out of the question for gays and lesbians as well as trans-men and trans-women. In addition to the racial superiority aspect, there is also a moral and cultural aspect to the wrath of white supremacy. Those who identify as LGBTQ+ are too often chastised and condemned as evil and immoral and less than human. This was clear when Lt. Governor Mark Robinson of North Carolina referred to homosexuality and transgenderism as "filth." It was evident when Senator Ted Cruz of the state of Texas referred to the Supreme Court's decision to legalize gay marriage as "one of the darkest hours in our country." This is the kind of ignorant, narrow-minded thinking that exists in aspects of our own leadership.

Laws prohibiting gays and lesbians from marrying those they love or serving their country in uniform are fortunately in effect no longer; however, countless states across the country continue to enact laws that blatantly discriminate against those in the LGBTQ+ community. Many states have passed laws allowing private institutions, including schools, universities, and health insurance companies, to discriminate. Particularly over the course of the Trump presidency, the number of anti-LGBTQ+ hate groups increased forty-three percent, rising from forty-nine groups in 2018 to seventy in 2019. As the Trump administration pursued its dangerous tirade of anti-LGBTQ+ policies, its only response to the rising hate was that it was only a mere exaggeration on the part of Democrats.

There are some who would express opposition to combining the historical struggles of people of color and those who identify as LGBTQ+. They will assert that skin color is not a choice, but sexual orientation and gender identity are choices indeed. Whether or not one is born gay or into the body of the wrong gender is truly beyond the point. What if identifying with LGBTQ+ is indeed a choice? Doesn't the Declaration of Independence and the Constitution guarantee the liberty to every American citizen to live and do as they please? Since this is so, who gives some the right to demonize or physically attack or murder those who live differently from them? Who gives some the right to declare those different from they are as inferior? Should my life or your life be attacked because of the house you or I choose to live in or the car you or I choose to drive or clothes you or I choose to wear? Should you or I be denied the basic necessities of life or be killed just because of who we are and that we are not choosing to live how the dominant culture would prefer us to live? Those who subscribe to bigotry could not care any less whether skin color or sexual orientation or gender identity are choices or not. The bottom line is inferiority, and those who see others as less than human will only develop excuse after excuse only to justify their own sense of superiority. Furthermore, just stating that some are allowed to live however they please in private but should not be regarded as equal citizens under the laws of this country is no longer a viable excuse to regard those citizens as second-class.

As stated before, white supremacy consists of far more than just the feeling of malice in one's heart for individuals who are either non-white or subscribes to different cultural and moral standards. It has brought about the deaths of thousands of Americans both black and white as well as members of the LGBTQ+ community. It has often led and continues to lead to great mental distress on the part of individuals as well as social unrest. When individuals choose to take a stand and speak out against the system, they are often deemed racist or accused of seeking to stir division.

Many conservatives will proclaim that those challenging injustice hate our country and should possibly leave. Some will simply dismiss certain systemic injustices and accuse people of color as simply trying to victimize themselves and be dependent on government. The same individuals will disregard the historical significance of certain forms of rhetoric and their impact upon various groups of Americans. Those who subscribe to this kind of thinking are driven only by the mantrum walls of their own reality. They are dangerously oblivious to any reality beyond their own and will proceed even to dismiss the realities of others without seeking to become more familiar with them. The fundamental problem is that there are too many in this country who subscribe to this kind of thinking; there are far too many of them serving in high positions of power at both the national and state levels.

White supremacy exists in more than just the institutions for which define our everyday lives. It influences the collective attitudes we as Americans share with one another pertaining to race and gender and sexual orientation. It is no question that "whiteness" is often deemed the dominant culture in America, which is also coined as "American" culture. There is also the false senses of toxic masculinity and feminism based on decades of white male cultural dominance. If an individual does not subscribe to a certain degree of "whiteness," they are often viewed as less than on the part of too many. This may consist of the young African American male who wears dreads or braids and loose-fitting clothes and listens to rap or hip-hop or a woman of any color or kind who chooses to embrace herself as a woman, given the shame that follows. Let us not forget the people of color who are often viewed as a threat for no valid reason by too many in law enforcement as well as society. The male who chooses to wear tight-fitting clothes will often be labeled as feminine or gay in the form of insults and belittlement, while the woman who may be seen dressed in tight-fitting or somewhat revealing clothes is often labeled a nymphomaniac and may be called even worse things. Let us not forget the elderly Asian-American walking on the sidewalk who is demonized because a disgraced former president could do no better than to blame a deadly virus on those who look like them. The gay couple seen walking down the street will be called an abomination and may be attacked or killed, while trans-women are often accused of being perverts who serve as a threat to children. Let us also acknowledge those who loves to wear black and portray a gothic persona who will be labeled an abomination or as devil worshippers.

All of this extends back to the limited scope of life based on a biased, closed-minded reality rooted in ignorance and hate. Julie Sondra Decker stated in her book *The Invisible Orientation* that "being a minority within a minority requires safety, conviction, and comfort within one's environment that is not always available to the more persecuted and oppressed people in Western society." Ms. Decker also stated that "Western society treats these groups as if they exist to perform certain functions for the majority rather than to have their own wants and needs." The reality is that various groups of Americans should not be required to subscribe to the dominant, white cisgender male culture to be respected as citizens and human beings. One should not be required to abandon their own sense of self or culture to avoid the historical stereotypes and the belittlement endured by their ancestors. One should not be forced to abandon who they are at heart to function in everyday society. Furthermore, embracing the growing diversity, multiculturalism, and inclusivity in society is no attempt to pursue a cultural revolution or make America into something she was never intended to be. Anyone who believes these untruths is not only part of the problem but possibly a subscriber to white supremacy.

Earlier I made the statement that white supremacist hatred for people of color and members of the LGBTQ+ community consists of fruits from the same poisonous tree. Those who subscribe to white supremacist doctrine perceive all of those who are not white, cisgender, and heterosexual as inferior for the same reason. The foundation beneath the racism that negatively impacted people of color for centuries consists of religion. In his first autobiography, Frederick Douglass spoke of his slave master, Thomas Auld, and his conversion to Christianity at a Methodist meeting. Douglass assumed that Auld's conversion would cleanse his heart and encourage him to free his slaves. Douglass accounted, however, that Auld became more hateful and racist. While he prayed day and night and practiced religious traditions faithfully, Auld would continue to practice the very evils in which Jesus Himself condemns. Frederick Douglass believed in "the widest possible difference" between the "slaveholding religion of this land" and "the pure, peaceable, and impartial Christianity of Christ."

I am someone who loves Christ with all my heart, and I strive to become more like Him each day. While the love of God is what defines my personal life, it also defines how I treat others, respond to adversity, and inspires me to build a better world in which for all of God's children to live. It inspires me to be there for those in need and fight for greater justice and opportunities on behalf of those who lack thereof. More importantly, the love of God guards my heart from evil and urges me to heavily condemn it when I encounter it. The love of Christ is intended for growth; it is meant to bring us all closer together and see one another. It is meant to build others in the name of humility and compassion. It is the act of discernment that must dictate not only our individual conscience but our collective conscience. Those who subscribe to white supremacist doctrine, however, applies and defends hate and injustice in the very name of our Creator and Savior. They will often use scriptural verses to justify bigotry and separation. No matter what you may look like, no matter who you love, and no matter the background from which you derive, God loves you. He loves us all the same, and He will never stand for the hate that seeks to divide and destroy His children.

Many will heavily condemn greater diversity, the act of abortion, and personal decisions that individuals make behind closed doors in the name of God's love and family values but turn a blind eye to poverty, systemic injustice, climate change, gun violence, and mental illness. Those who are offended by the movement to establish greater equality while turning a blind eye to the evils that plague millions of lives each day are not pro-life nor pro-family nor Christian but just a huge part of the problem in America today. All of those who truly seek to live like Jesus and honor what is good and decent in our humanity would never condone racial or cultural superiority of any kind. They would never manipulate the Word of God to judge, belittle, and demonize others while calling themselves Christians. They would also take a firm stand in the face of evils such as the unlawful murders of unarmed people of color as well as the physical and verbal harassment of gays and lesbians and trans-men and trans-women. Those who are heavily offended when white supremacy is condemned as well as the injustices that are the result may just very well subscribe to this philosophy altogether. If this is true, they would be adhering to what Frederick Douglass called "the slaveholding religion" and not the abiding love and impeccable character of Jesus Christ. Under no circumstance would Christ condone the mistreatment of others in the forms of greed, ignorance, hate, and discrimination.

Do not refer to yourself as a Christian if you are not outraged and willing to take a stand when people of color and members of the LGBTQ+ community are assaulted and killed in the name of hate and bigotry. Do not store various sins on a pedestal while turning a blind conscience to the sins that harm us as a collective. Do not manipulate the perfect love of God to justify your own hate and intolerance of those who are different from you. Furthermore, those who truly honor who we are as Americans would never subscribe to an arrogant, closed-minded ideology that denounces growth and improvement and condemns those who put forth an analysis of the state of our nation. As the roaring lion of white supremacy continues to ravage across our nation like a devil on steroids, Americans of every kind must rise together and work more diligently than ever to rid this evil from our DNA. This will be easier said than done, but we owe it to ourselves. We owe it to our children; we owe it to all the generations of Americans to come.

During efforts to create a society that is fairer and more equal for all, those who live under white supremacist doctrine will often ask the question "what about me?" or "what about a holiday or a movement for my race?" or make statements such as "well they already have these privileges so why aren't they satisfied?" Followers of white supremacist doctrine will also accuse minorities of seeking out special treatment and failing to take responsibility for their own well-being. Concerning the LGBTQ+ community, those who subscribe to white supremacist doctrine will often argue on behalf of a month honoring "straight pride" or "male pride." Historically, those who happen to be white, male, straight, and cisgender have not endured systemic discrimination and hate crimes on such a large and disproportionate scale in contrast to people of color and those who identify as part of the LGBTQ+ community.

All of those who have not endured widespread injustice throughout history have never had to fight and sacrifice each day of their lives for the basic right of merely existing and functioning in everyday society. They were never disowned by their families and made homeless because of their race or sexual orientation or gender identity. They were never assaulted or killed in record numbers simply because of what they look like or who they are. Minorities and many in the LGBTQ+ community have endured all these harsh realities, and certainly holidays and movements exist to not only remember their struggles but honor their strides. Those who are truly educated and open-minded and seek to live in a society where no individual is treated poorly due to a shallow premise will never ask the question "what about me" but "what can I do on my part to better understand the realities beyond that of my own and put an end to hate and intolerance in all their forms?" Instead of those in the dominant group choosing to complain too often about movements and initiatives ought to be grateful that they never needed them in the first place.

We must march and protest in the streets peacefully but firmly and loudly; we must vote in every election from local to national in record numbers; we must mobilize in our neighborhoods and communities like we never have before. Let us begin the work of scaling back the radical Far Right efforts to revive the era of Jim Crow and ensure that every citizen regardless of race have the right to vote and participate in our democracy by making the Freedom to Vote and John Lewis Voting Rights Advancement Acts the laws of the land. Let us fight side by side to eliminate systemic injustices in employment, education, housing, healthcare, law enforcement treatment, and prison sentencing. We must never stop until all those who pursue injustice are held fully accountable by law and that all Americans regardless of background are no longer disregarded and degraded because of who they are and where they come from. We must continue to fight for our gay and lesbian and transgender sisters and brothers and strive steadfast until the Equality Act is the law of the land.

The time of standing idly by and making the same decade-old excuses again and again must come to an end. We as Americans must strive wholeheartedly until every tenet of white supremacy ceases to exist. The only way this can happen is for those who subscribe to the tenets of this evil ideology have absolutely no influence in policy and American politics altogether. Only when the sin of hate is abolished in its entirety will we truly live up to our collective identity and full potential as the American people.

8

THE PUBLIC TRUST

One of the greatest privileges of being an American is enjoying the freedom to choose those who will represent us in the halls of power. Upon the ratification of the Constitution, our Founders designed a system of government that would prevent the accumulation of unprecedented authority. Affording each citizen the power of choosing our nation's leaders was a probable factor in preventing the accumulation of too much power. The American people carry out this privilege every two to four years when deciding who will represent them in either the White House or Congress or in their own state as governor or in the state legislature. Unfortunately, some Americans had to sacrifice and fight with their lives in securing their right to have a voice in democracy. African Americans and women from every background fought for decades for a right that was given to them by the Constitution. While there are many who are attempting to take away this right for mere political purposes, all Americans enjoy the privilege of choosing who will best represent their voices in democracy.

Every election victory is met with enormous celebration filled with deep emotions and glorious triumph. Eventually the loud applauses will wane, the shouting will calm, the victory parties will wind down, and the campaign paraphernalia goes on the shelf. Afterwards, most of us return to normal life with the expectation that our newly elected leaders will accomplish the goals in which we entrusted them to accomplish. Some of these leaders offer greater promises than others; some will apply greater oratory than others in uttering those promises. As a couple of years progress, we may realize that many of these promises will never become reality. The minimum wage remains below the cost of living, our schools fail to meet the educational needs of our children, there are no greater opportunities in which for many of us to rise from the depths of poverty, our infrastructure continues to crumble, the longevity of our planet continues to slip away due to a warming climate, and the laws in which govern the purchase of firearms remain the same. As time proceeds, the great people of this country see little to no progress regarding the vital things that dictate our everyday lives. Some will eventually grow wary of the political process and abandon hope for its prospects altogether.

The purpose of leadership is doing for the people those things in which they cannot do for themselves. This is the reason we have the system of government in America in which we do. Our leaders are entrusted with the responsibility of increasing the quality of life for the citizens in which they represent. Our leaders are responsible for reforming the iniquities that make life more difficult than it must be. Whether one is Democrat, Republican, liberal, or conservative, a simpler, more equal, and more modernized way of life is desired by the American people and certainly well within reach. The only thing that gets in the way too often is the failure of our political leaders in fulfilling their intended goals. It is the betrayal on the part of elected officials to do what they were entrusted to do, which is serve those who elected them by doing what they cannot do for themselves. Raising the minimum wage, reforming our education system, protecting human rights, honoring a woman's right to choose, prolonging the longevity of our planet, and instituting both reasonable and sound gun control are fundamental obligations that all leaders should be able to accomplish with no problems. Any reason that our leaders develop to not do what they know will increase the quality of life is nothing more than an excuse to not do so. It is an absolute disgrace and betrayal when those we entrust with power choose to not act in a moment of unprecedented crisis.

The more our leaders in both parties continue with endless fighting and bickering, the more leaders blame one another for the major problems in our country, the more we portray the other side as the enemy, and the more we continue the path of inaction, the deeper we as a country will dig ourselves into. Most Americans only desire the basic things out of life. They desire to a livable wage to support their household. They desire the ability to raise their children by giving them the things they never had growing up. This is how they give them a greater life than they had growing up. This is how the American Dream lives on. When leaders run for public office and reach victory, they have achieved the trust of those who chose to elect them. Trust is everything in the world when one seems to have nothing left and few people to depend on. When one has been deceived and betrayed time and time again after so long, they begin to doubt their own truth. The denial of this truth causes great distress and pain upon those who work truly hard each day just to give their children a life better than they had. It causes major uncertainly and void among those who may think it is their fault and wonder if the circumstances may ever shift in their favor.

As so many Americans continue to doubt the truth of our greatness at no fault of their own after years of corruption and inaction, they may decide to stay at home and not vote during the next upcoming election. Is it their fault? Are they wrong? Or is it fault of those who have lied and proven themselves to be unresourceful time and time again? It is the fault of those who have failed to live up to the ideals of our Founding Fathers who sought to extend to future generations a government that would serve the people over the self-interests that serve as a threat to their well-being. Most Americans desire to give their children the lives they never had, and this is primarily the reason they vote. Any leader who betrays those Americans who desire the simpler things to the point where they desire to not vote is only complicit in the erosion of our democracy. While it is a great tragedy for any

American to not express their right to vote, it is an even greater tragedy when politicians give them a reason to not do so. It is a tragedy in and of itself to betray the public trust.

It is beyond hypocritical for politicians to reinforce the importance of voting every election cycle but fail deliberately and miserably in fulfilling their duties to the people who elected them. For politicians to do the people's work would be fulfilling the promise of our Founders. It would be honoring the sacrifices made by many in making our nation a more perfect union. Part of never forgetting our Founders or the people we come from is allowing them to live on through us and our children. Sometimes we can only begin journeys that our offspring must finish. Our Founders started this journey called America; it is up to us to keep it going. I strongly encourage all of those who have lost faith in our leaders to never give up. Do not abandon hope for what America can and must accomplish. If you are one of those who are beyond dissatisfied with the division and lack of progress, gather with your fellow Americans and forge a political movement to bring about progress on the issues important to you and your community. Forge a movement to bring about greater opportunities and equal treatment for all Americans and reverse all efforts to take our country back into the 1950s.

This country belongs to the individuals who work hard each day in service to us all. America belongs to those who black, white, Hispanic, Asian, and Native American. It belongs to those who are gay, straight, cisgender, transgender, and non-binary. It belongs to the moms and dads, daughters and sons, sisters and brothers, aunts and uncles, and grandmothers and grandfathers. It belongs to the teachers and professors, doctors and nurses, cops and firefighters, and those working entry-level jobs just to keep afloat. The goal of our leaders should be to establish a system where Americans do not have to work as hard just to have to basic things out of life. It is to ensure that Americans from every walk of life can feed and support their families without having to sacrifice all that which is vital to fully achieving the American Dream.

The time is now that our elected leaders stop taking the American people for granted and start living up to their constitutional and moral obligations. The time is now for our leaders to fulfill their responsibilities to the citizens who elect them and do all that is required to make life simpler somewhat so that future generations are not forced to work and sacrifice harder than they must. The public trust is vital to not only the future of our economy but our democracy. If we begin the work now of healing our country from decades of corruption and inaction, we can not only heal our democracy from dangerous wounds but put our country on the path to true prosperity that will endure for generations to come.

CONCLUSION

What you have just explored is a passionate analysis concerning the crisis in our democracy and the meltdown of the former party of Lincoln. There is no question that the Republican Party has abandoned the ideals and principles it once hailed as sacred. A newfound radicalism of the Far Right built on lies and division and baseless conspiracy theories has infiltrated the core of the base of the G.O.P. The Republican Party has sold its soul to Donald Trump as if he is a spiritual deity, and it will wholeheartedly condemn any party member who expresses opposition. "What would Trump do?" is the party's new moral compass. As stated in the second chapter, the ultimate outcome of Trumpism is civil war. Civil war happens when our nation becomes so far gone in divisive tension to the point where we can no longer see each other as one American people. The bad news is that too many Republican leaders are continuing to aid and abed Donald Trump and the toxic machine without conscience. The good news, however, is that there is a substantial number of unheard conservative Republicans who did in fact reject Trumpism wholeheartedly.

There were many lifelong Republican voters and some serving in power who have left the party altogether because they saw what had become of the party that was taken away from them. I know this to be true because….. I was one of them. This is something that I considered strongly of not sharing with others because I am honestly ashamed and disappointed to have once considered myself a Republican. After long hours of thinking and consulting with friends, I concluded that sharing my former allegiance to the Republican Party would have a positive impact because it demonstrates that anyone has the ability to reject indecency and toxic mechanisms. It also demonstrates that anyone has the power to become better educated concerning the issues and the unfortunate realities that exist in our world, which is something the former party of Lincoln has no longer.

I was someone who was elated by some of the ideas of family values and individual initiative. I would declare strongly that our faith in God should dictate our personal character and inspire us to be good to others. I spoke positively concerning the ideals of self-government and leading through strength in the global arena. However, I came to realize that all of these are principles that Americans in both parties hold to be sacred. Democrats and Republicans alike believe in liberty and strong families and the ability to do for ourselves. Most of us love God and believe that we should treat one another with kindness and respect. None of us are any more or less patriotic because of our beliefs. Anyone who would demonize fellow Americans who happen to share different views are complicit in our national division. Furthermore, I decided that I could no longer remain in the party that refuses to acknowledge or address systemic racism or any other unfortunate reality that affects certain groups of Americans.

As I witnessed the former President's failed handling of the COVID-19 pandemic and his disgraceful response to the civil unrest that took place last summer, I was not only disgusted and appalled but gravely disappointed. I was far more angered and furious to see so many conservative Republicans remain silent in the face of racial injustice but become offended when Americans of all races took a stand against it. Seeing the former President and so many in his base demonstrate profound and shameful disregard for a deadly pandemic was embarrassing on the world stage. To see the former President and so many in the Republican Party demonstrate a strong lack of compassion for human life and stand at ease with racist, hateful rhetoric were the absolute dealbreakers for me. I was done. As a person who does the best to live a life of moral decency, I was able to stand tall and declare that all I had witnessed was profoundly wrong. There was absolutely no way I could support another dark and toxic four years. There was absolutely no way I could continue to call myself a conservative and remain in the former party of Lincoln.

Simply standing up for what is right should have nothing to do with one's political views or affiliation; it is a basic human reflex in the face of evil and indecency. If someone is walking down the street and encounters someone laying on the ground, his or her first instinct is to call for help or attempt to perform CPR or ask the person if he or she is ok. One's political views should not stop him or her from calling out evil. The fact that so many Republicans failed to apply this basic human reflex to the dark leadership of Donald Trump only demonstrates a great deal of how far we as a country has digressed. No human being should ever allow their self to be conned and morally compromised to the point where admiration for a political figure replaces moral conscience and love for country. This only leads to greater acts of evil without consequence.

What is far more deplorable is the consistent attempt of the radical Far Right to accuse the media of slandering what it is and what it represents. Any individual who has common sense knows very well that words have consequences. When someone steps in front of a camera or goes on social media and makes statements that are either hateful or cannot be proven to be true, there will always be consequences. People are listening and watching. People hear the shallow comments and jokes degrading who they are because of their race or gender or sexual orientation. People are listening when radical Far Right politicians and journalists attack their culture or ethnicity or country of origin. The American people watched and listened for two months as blatant election lies were spread, which ultimately led to violence and death.

We all hear the narrow-minded rhetoric that remains historically inaccurate and dangerously insensitive to the various realities of the world we all live in. Not only does America hear, but we condemn the hate and ignorance and hold those individuals accountable. If one does not enjoy being scolded by the media or labeled as racist or xenophobic or misogynistic, he or she should not go in front of a camera or on social media and make statements and comments that are indeed hateful and that disregard facts and reality and underscore human decency. The same individual would never put his or her foot in his or her mouth consistently and get offended when the world tries to put its foot someplace else. When you demonstrate a profound disregard for our common humanity and start to endure the heat, do not call the rest of us politically correct or blame the media for calling you out; blame yourself and take responsibility for your own carelessness and hate. Get your head out of the clouds and put an end to the nonsense once and for all or you will be left behind in your own limited scope of life.

I challenge all of those on the Far Right who refer to themselves as Christians to consider something for a second. Do you worship Jesus Christ or Donald Trump? What would Jesus Christ say about Donald Trump? How long will it take for you to denounce this newfound toxic machine known as Trumpism? How much more violence and loss of life must occur? How many more insurrections on our Capitol must occur? How divided and broken must our democracy become? At what point will you decide it is time to address systemic injustice and meet the threats to our planet? Would Jesus stand idly by and allow more and more hardworking Americans slip into poverty and despair at no fault of their own? What must happen for you to be able to stand up and say "enough is enough!"? If rejecting the evil that has befallen our republic is so difficult, I know where your heart lies, and it is not with the heart of Christ. I also know where your loyalty lies, and it is not with your fellow Americans. The heart of Jesus is strong and powerful enough to reject Trumpism with no shame because it is the right thing to do, and love of country should propel all of us to reject all that would destroy our proud land just to get what it wants. This is what our moral DNA summons upon each of us to do, in addition to abolishing discrimination and building greater opportunities for every American citizen.

For one to be anti-abortion, anti-women, anti-LGBTQ+, and a believer in capitalism but blatantly refuses to address systemic racism, dismisses the threats of climate change as a hoax, finds every reason to not support a livable wage and greater opportunities for all Americans, and refuses to reject toxic leadership does not make them pro-life and certainly does not make them Christian. What it makes that person is just a bigger part of the problem. All those individuals will have a rude awakening on Judgment Day when they stand before the Lord and declare how much they loved Him when they lived on Earth. They will brag strongly about how well they fought to restrict access to abortion and how well they sought to punish the LGBTQ+ community for being sinful. They will also boast about all they had done to fulfill the Lord's work. The Lord will look at each of them and say as He did in Matthew 7:23, "I never knew you. Depart from me."

As a Christian, I use my faith and my love for God to become a greater person every morning I wake up. My faith in Christ and abiding love for our Creator are not based on a set of beliefs. They are based on the way we treat one another as God's children. They are based on our behavior and the things we do that affect others on a broad scale. They dictate our conscience as well as our efforts to improve the world we live in through erasing evil and injustice. The life of Christ is an example of how each of us should strive to be each day that passes by. The Christian faith should guide the urgency to reverse the ills that inflict harm and pain upon the most vulnerable. It should spread peace and bring all of God's children closer together. My faith does not implore me to belittle and condemn all that which is the opposite of my own beliefs and culture. With all that being said, it is time that our friends on the Far Right stop using the example of Christ and the love of God as tools to spread bigotry and hate. I have some idea who the radical Far Right worships as God but it is not the One who gave His life on the Cross and loves all of His children the same.

It is time for the Republican Party to stop worshipping Donald J. Trump and, again, get off the bandwagon of closed-minded thinking, hate speech, and the spread of misinformation. It needs to come on board with the rest of the country so we can move forward. If the party truly refuses to do so, it needs to step aside. If it does not step aside and chooses to remain this toxic cult that worships Donald Trump, we may just lose what we know as the United States of America. None of us as Americans should want that for ourselves nor for our posterity. To elect Donald Trump in 2024 as our nation's leader once again would put our nation on the most dangerously unprecedented path that any of us could ever imagine. The morally tragic events of before rests greatly in contrast to what will happen if we return to the previous era, and the former party of Lincoln will seal its place in history as the enablers of democracy's demise.